Will Man Survive?

Will Man Survive?

PROPHECY YOU CAN UNDERSTAND

by

J. Dwight Pentecost

MOODY PRESS
CHICAGO

ISBN: 0-8024-9558-3

Fourth Printing, 1974

Library of Congress Catalog Card Number: 70-155687

Printed in the United States of America

To Jane
with a father's love

CONTENTS

1

PROPHECY AND DAILY LIVING

SEVERAL YEARS AGO I was invited to a downtown office building to teach a Bible class. It was just prior to the Six-Day War, and I was to speak on prophecy and the significance of current events in the light of prophecy. I took the occasion to survey events of the end time as revealed in the Word of God to show how current events are preparatory for the final drama leading up to Christ's enthronement as David's Son on David's throne.

At the conclusion of the message a woman said, "In the light of your study, it seems to me that the coming of the Lord Jesus must be very, very near. I have some dirty closets at home that I must clean out, for I would not want the Lord to come and take me home to Himself and have somebody come in and find the closets the way they are now." That is the practical effect of prophecy on daily life. For not only in our homes but in our lives are many dirty, crowded nooks and crannies that need to be cleaned out. I would like to discuss in a practical way the subject of the practical effects of prophecy.

Some skeptics feel that anyone interested in studying prophecy is mentally unbalanced. They think prophetic studies are for those of low intellectual ability. Those who study the prophetic portions of the Word are put in the class of the Athenians of whom Paul testified in Acts 17:21 that "all the Athenians and strangers which were there spent their time in nothing else, but either to tell, or to hear some new thing."

Obviously many open the prophetic Scriptures simply to stir the imagination or to emphasize the spectacular. But prophecy plays an important part in God's program. One-fourth of the books of Scripture fall into the classification of prophetic books. One verse out of five deals with some subject that was prophetic at the time it was written. Ignorance of such a large body of divine truth means ignorance of many of God's purposes and programs. The very fact that prophecy is there gives warrant for studying and knowing it. But there are certain practical effects too. It has been quite evident, especially since the Middle East conflagration began, that one of the most practical results of the knowledge of the prophetic Word is that it gives assurance in difficult, troubled and trying days. It provides a foundation on which to build, something on which to stand. A pastor in northern New Jersey wrote at the time of the Six-Day War: "I have been studying your book on prophecy. For a long time I believed as you do in a pretribulational rapture in which Christ would appear in the clouds to take believers to Himself. But I'm all confused and shaken up, for Palestine is in the hands of the Israelis and even Jerusalem is now occupied by Israel. Doesn't that mean that the times of the Gentiles have already ended? When the times of the Gentiles end we should be with the Lord. I think I will have to abandon the position that I had held all these years." This person was shaken in his beliefs because he was unable to relate current events to the total revealed program and see them in their true light. This principle can be illustrated in Genesis 18 in a brief incident in Abraham's life. Abraham, who was called the friend of God, had walked with God and received His promises and covenants. God had not withheld anything that He purposed to do from Abraham. Suppose you had been in Abraham's shoes. You had been living with God as Abraham lived with Him, and suddenly the heavens opened and fire and brimstone poured down on two of the most prominent cities of the world in that day until they were totally destroyed. There was no human explanation for it and you knew that God had done it. What do you suppose you would ask God? "Why did this happen? Can You explain this to me?" Your faith in God would be shaken because you were ignorant of what God was doing. Before God judged the wicked cities of Sodom and Gomorrah, He prepared Abraham to witness that event so that he would have confidence in Him and understand what was taking place when it happened. The Lord said, "Shall I hide from Abraham that thing which I do?" (Gen 18:17). In effect, He said, "I have no secret to keep from My friend Abraham. I don't want him to be confused, perplexed and upset when this conflagration comes on Sodom and Gomorrah. Therefore I will tell him beforehand so that when it comes he will know that it is all according to My plan and purpose." So God spelled out in detail to Abraham exactly what He was going to do. The fact that God moved according to a revealed program left Abraham unshaken and unmoved when he witnessed the total destruction of Sodom and Gomorrah. A great part of his world was being wiped out because those cities had had such an influence in that area. In a stroke they were taken away. But Abraham continued to walk with God; His faith in God was unshaken. This catastrophe never caused him to doubt God's character or purposes or to doubt his own safety and security. He could move through the judgment in perfect rest and peace because God had revealed it all to him beforehand.

In John 13 the most significant event in the world's history was about to take place. Christ was about to be crucified. That death would mean a separation from the disciples. His body would be placed in a grave—the first separation from them. Then He would be restored to them by resurrection, but after a brief interval He would ascend into heaven—a second separation. How did He prepare the disciples for these separations? He said, "Now I tell you before it come, that, when it is come to pass, ye may believe that I am he" (Jn 13:19). When death laid hold of Christ, why didn't the disciples renounce Him? Because He had told them ahead of time exactly what was going to happen. When He was sealed in the tomb, why didn't they forsake Him? Because He had told them exactly what would happen. In obedience to His command they tarried in the upper room until He came to them after His resurrection. Christ took them into His confidence concerning the prophetic program as it related to them so that they would not doubt His person and His power, nor the program that He had come to fulfill.

I was profoundly satisfied and joyful that when something as earthshaking in its prophetic significance as the Six-Day War happened, those whom I had taught the Word were not moved, shaken, in despair, distraught or perplexed, wondering what was going on. They could fit it into God's program because they understood the prophetic Scriptures. I do not know of any time in all of my ministry when the expectation that the Lord might come at anytime was as high and real to Christians as it has been in these past months. That is the practical result of knowing the prophetic Scriptures. We are not strangers to God. We are His friends and, as His friends, He has taken us into His confidence as to what He is going to do; and with His guidebook, the Bible, we can walk through the battlefield, knowing the end that He has determined.

Another practical result of understanding prophecy is that the expectation that Christ might come for His saints at anytime provides more incentive to labor in His name than perhaps any other truth in God's Word. In 1 Thessalonians 4—5, Paul, in dealing with the truths concerning Christ's coming, speaks of the practical result of this truth in a believer's life:

> But of the times and the seasons, brethren, ye have no need that I write unto you. For yourselves know perfectly that the day of the Lord so cometh as a thief in the night (1 Th 5:1-2).

He will come unannounced and unheralded, when He is least expected. A thief who is going to enter a home does not send a message announcing that he is on his way, revealing the time of his arrival. He comes unheralded and unexpected. While many signs announce to the world that Christ is returning to earth to reign after the tribulation, no signs will tell believers when He is coming in the clouds of glory to translate us to Himself before the tribulation begins.

> For yourselves know perfectly that the day of the Lord so cometh as a thief in the night. For when they shall say, Peace and safety; then sudden destruction cometh upon them, as travail upon a woman with child; and they shall not escape (vv. 2-3).

Paul says unbelievers who hear the truths that Christ could come at any moment will turn away and scoff when they see events preparing for the final drama; they will be unmoved by them because of their ignorance of God's Word. He says that to such as are in ignorance, there will come a judgment as sudden as labor pains come upon a woman with child, and they shall not escape. Then he addresses a word to believers:

> But ye, brethren, are not in darkness [that is, in ignorance], that that day should overtake you as a thief. Ye are all the children of light, and the children of the day: we are not of the night, nor of the darkness. Therefore, let us not sleep (vv. 4-6).

The word *therefore* is significant because it gives the logical conclusion or application of the truth just stated. Because believers can know the prophetic Scriptures and see how the parts of prophecy fit together, we are not "to sleep," which here indicates indolence and cessation of all activity. He exhorts,

> Let us watch and be sober. For they that sleep sleep in the night; and they that be drunken are drunken in the night. But let us, who are of the day, be sober (vv. 6-8).

And the word "sober" means serious-minded, giving attention to things in the light of reality. We are to be

> putting on the breastplate of faith and love; and for an helmet, the hope of salvation. For God hath not appointed us to wrath, but to obtain salvation by our Lord Jesus Christ (vv. 8-9).

Paul is emphasizing that those who have this blessed hope that the Lord could come at any moment to translate us into glory will be men who are awake, active, and doing the work that God has assigned them because the night is coming when no man can work. Those were Christ's words in John 9:4 where He said, when confronted by the man born blind, "I must work the works of him that sent me, while it is day: the night cometh, when no man can work." The Lord realized there was a time to labor and there would be a time when there would be no opportunity to labor. So Paul emphasizes in 1 Thessalonians that in the light of the truth of Christ's coming, we are to labor in His name. This truth is emphasized again in Ephesians 5:14-15:

> Wherefore he saith, Awake thou that sleepest, and arise from the dead, and Christ shall give thee light. See then that ye walk circumspectly, not as fools but as wise, redeeming the time, because the days are evil.

The word *circumspectly* means "looking all around you." The phrase *redeeming the time* might be translated "buying up the opportunities." That which will terminate the opportunity is Christ's coming to take believers home to Himself. Paul is saying, "While God gives you an opportunity, avail yourselves of it, because the days are evil." A man is unwise when he cannot see his present situation in its true light. If we could ignore all the evidences God has given that the end of the age is approaching, then we could afford to be indifferent because we could say there is still much time to do the work that God has entrusted us to do. But when we see events in the light of the Word, we understand what God's will is, and have a responsibility to redeem the time.

In writing 2 Thessalonians, the apostle had to deal in a practical way with the matter of indolence. He had taught them in his first letter that Christ was coming for the saints, and in that day those saints believed just as much as believers do today that the Lord Jesus might appear while they were still alive to translate them into glory. This is what is called the imminent hope: that the Lord could come at any moment. Paul believed Christ could come in his day; believers in Thessalonica believed He might come in their day; and John, the last of the apostles, believed He might be coming in his day. The saints down through the ages have believed it as well. But after these Thessalonians had received that truth, they became indolent, sat down to wait, and gave themselves over to laziness. In 2 Thessalonians, Paul deals with this problem by reminding them that he was an example to them. While as an apostle he might have been supported by them, he worked so that they wouldn't have to pay his support. But then he reminds them, "Even when we were with you, this we commanded you, that if any would not work, neither should he eat" (3:10). These people were content to live off the rest of the Christians, who, while believing that the Lord was coming, still worked at their daily jobs and came home with their wages. The believers who had spent the day in laziness went to the saints who worked and borrowed necessities from them. Thus they were living off the working saints. Paul said that "if any would not work, neither should he eat. For we hear that there are some which walk among you disorderly, working not at all, but are busybodies. Now them that are such we command and exhort by our Lord Jesus Christ, that with quietness they work, and eat their own bread. But ye, brethren, be not weary in well doing" (vv. 10-13). In other words, he was saying, "You believe that the Lord is coming. Fine. You believe that He might come today? So do I." But he adds, "That shouldn't keep you from being on the job so that when the day closes you'll have your pay to take home to provide your daily bread to eat. You have a responsibility to work while you wait." We have a responsibility to live today as though the Lord might come before we go to bed, but to plan for tomorrow as though He wouldn't come for a hundred years. In conducting our church business or individual business, we must live with the hope that Christ might come at anytime, but to plan as though He would not come for one hundred years. Thus, the study of prophecy stirs the saints to activity, to be busy in the Lord's business until He comes.

In 1 Corinthians 16:22 Paul writes, "If any man love not the Lord Jesus Christ, let him be Anathema Maran-atha." The word *anathema* means "accursed." It is the word that had to do with imposing a judgment on one who is guilty. "Maran-atha" means "our Lord cometh." This suggests that when Paul used the word *Maran-atha* he was reminding the saints that they were to conduct themselves and the affairs in the assembly in the light of the truth that the Lord Jesus Christ was coming. His coming will bring judgment on those who are anathema. It is as though Paul said, "Don't let the Lord come and find a group associated with your assembly that has no business being here. You conduct your affairs in the light of the fact that Maran-atha, the Lord is coming." When the saints in New Testament times used to greet each other, they did not say "Hello" or shake hands. When one saint met another, he said, "Maran-atha, the Lord is coming." They were living their lives in the light of the hope that the Lord Jesus might come at any moment. What a wonderful thing to greet one another with such a word as that, a constant reminder that the Lord is coming.

While the Word associates many things with the truth of the Lord's return, such as incentive, comfort, and knowledge, the most common usage is an exhortation to holiness. Above all else, it was designed to produce holiness. The apostle John referred to this in 1 John 3:3, "And every man that hath this hope in him [that is, centered in Christ, does what?] purifieth himself, even as he is pure." The practical result of a study of biblical prophecy should be to promote holiness in daily life. It is impossible to find a reference to Christ's second coming in the epistles that does not couple with that doctrine an exhortation to holiness or godliness. Every time the New Testament writers refer to Christ's coming, there is a "therefore"—an exhortation to holiness. See what Peter does with it:

> Seeing then that all these things shall be dissolved, what manner of persons ought ye to be in all holy conversation [manner of life] and godliness, looking for and hasting unto the coming of the day of God, wherein the heavens being on fire shall be dissolved, and the elements shall melt with fervent heat? Nevertheless we, according to his promise, look for new heavens and a new earth, wherein dwelleth righteousness. Wherefore, beloved, seeing that ye look for such things, be diligent that ye may be found of him in peace, without spot, and blameless (2 Pe 3:11-14).

In Titus 2, Paul writes,

> For the grace of God that bringeth salvation hath appeared to all men, teaching us that, denying ungodliness and worldly lusts, we should live soberly, righteously, and godly, in this present world: [while we are] looking for that blessed hope, and the glorious appearing of the great God and our Saviour Jesus Christ (vv. 11-13).

We should live "soberly, righteously, and godly, in this present world [while we are] looking for that blessed hope." Passage after passage could be given, but these are sufficient to bring home the truth that God has revealed His prophetic program not to satisfy our curiosity; not only to give us hope, comfort, assurance, or an incentive to labor; but that these truths may produce godliness, righteousness, and purity of life in us while we are waiting for Christ's return. There is no greater deterrent to misconduct in a child than to tell him as you leave the room, "I'll be back in a minute." The expectation of a parent's return will keep that child from his desired course of action. Christ has promised, "I'll be back in a minute. It won't be long." And the child of God cries as John cried at the close of the Revelation: "Even so come, Lord Jesus." But no child of God who is living in sin can pray that prayer or voice that plea, "Even so come," for what child of God enmeshed in sin would think of inviting the Lord Jesus to come and see him in that transgression? The fact that Christ could come at any moment was designed to produce a purity and a holiness of life. As believers derive joy, hope, comfort, assurance and an incentive to serve God from the prophetic Word, may they also have the purity of life that it was designed to produce.

2

THE MINISTRY OF THE PROPHET

IN THE OLD TESTAMENT, three important offices were filled by divine appointment: those of priest, prophet, and king. The priest was a divinely appointed representative of men before God. The king was a divinely appointed ruler for God. The prophet was a divinely appointed spokesman to men for God. These three often worked together so that a full revelation might be given from God to man.

The priest operated in the religious realm as a mediator—one who offered sacrifices to God so that sinful men might have a covering for their sin. This was necessary because men were sinners. But men were not only sinners, they were lawless, and they needed to be ruled. God alone has the right to rule, so God appointed kings who should rule in His stead in order that lawlessness might be curbed. But men were not only sinners and lawless, they were ignorant and they needed a word from God—instruction concerning God. So God sent the prophet to deal with the problem of ignorance. Through the ministry of priest, king and prophet, God's will and way were made known to man.

It would be difficult to evaluate these three positions to determine which would be the most important, for they operated in different spheres and each was important. But in the present study of some of the major themes of prophecy, attention is directed to the prophet's ministry in order to understand his message and the purpose for this prophetic office. The prophet was primarily a spokesman for God to his generation. He was not removed from his generation or from his society, sitting in an ivory tower, gazing into a crystal ball, and occasionally astounding people with pronouncements concerning the future. He was grappling with current problems and current issues. The prophetic books of the Old Testament reveal that what the prophet had to say about things far removed from his time comprised a small part of his ministry. He was primarily a preacher, and his ministry was not so much one of consolation as one of condemnation. No wonder no one coveted the prophetic ministry, for if a prophet delivered the message that God gave him and condemned his society and generation, he of necessity would be most unpopular; and unpopularity was as unwanted in those days as it is today. The prophets often dealt with social issues, and condemned men on these grounds. They dealt with problems of immorality and revealed the standards of God's holiness. They dealt with the problems of drunkenness and condemned the overuse of wine. They condemned the oppression of the poor, the fatherless, and the widow. They condemned unjust extortion and interest rates, and taxation where it was not due. They condemned greed and avarice. They condemned businessmen for using false weights and improper balances. It may be surprising that the prophets became so concerned about these social issues, but they were very much involved in those pressing problems of their day.

They were involved in moral and religious issues as well as social issues, for they condemned idolatry, lawlessness, hypocrisy, and the substitution of men's words for God's word. They dealt with political issues, giving instruction concerning foreign alliances, and warning about trusting surrounding nations for deliverance from judgments that would come from God. Often the prophet made himself very unpopular, as Jeremiah did when he told the people that God was going to raise up a captor who would destroy Jerusalem, and they were not to resist. He told them to submit to this captor because he was a disciplinarian from the hand of God. The present-day relevance of the prophets' message is amazing.

But they are so relevant because, while times and customs have changed, men have not changed; and men manifest the sinfulness of the human heart today just as they did two or three thousand years ago. Obviously, thousands of years ago men had discovered all the ways of sinning that could be discovered and, while we try to improve sin in the present day, we haven't advanced it very far. The prophets were dealing with the sinful heart of man, condemning it for what it was. Many passages illustrate this emphasis in the prophets' preaching. Isaiah 1 gives an example of the prophet preaching about the religious and moral conditions of his day. Notice that he says nothing about the future; he is thundering a message of condemnation and judgment:

> Hear, O heavens, and give ear, O earth: for the LORD hath spoken, I have nourished and brought up children, and they have rebelled against me. The ox knoweth his owner, and the ass his master's crib: but Israel doth not know, my people doth not consider (vv. 2-3).

In present-day language, the prophet is saying, "You don't have the sense of an ox or ass. Any domesticated animal knows enough to respond when the master calls to feed it, and you don't know enough to do that." Isaiah describes their religious sins:

> Ah sinful nation, a people laden with iniquity, a seed of evildoers, children that are corrupters: they have forsaken the LORD, they have provoked the Holy One of Israel unto anger, they are gone away backward (v. 4).

Then he describes the emptiness of their religiosity:

> To what purpose is the multitude of your sacrifices unto me? saith the LORD: I am full of the burnt offerings of rams, and the fat of fed beasts; and I delight not in the blood of bullocks, or of lambs, or of he goats. When ye come to appear before me, who hath required this at your hand, to tread my courts? Bring no more vain oblations; incense is an abomination unto me; the new moons and sabbaths, the

> calling of assemblies, I cannot away with; it is iniquity, even the solemn meeting (vv. 11-13).

The prophet is saying just this: the nation has rebelled against God. The people are too deaf to hear the voice of God, and God counts all of their religious observances an empty abomination in His sight. Isaiah was doing the work of a prophet. He wasn't predicting something to come; he was convicting them of their need of repentance and forgiveness.

A New Testament prophet and his message are contained in Matthew. John the Baptizer appeared as a prophet with a prophetic message: "But when he saw many of the Pharisees and Sadducees come to his baptism, he said unto them, O generation of vipers . . ." (Mt 3:7-9). Or, in modern parlance, he looked at them and said, "You snakes in the grass. You talk about being rightly related to God. Let's see the fruit of repentance. Bring forth fruit meet for repentance." In Luke 3:12-13, when the publicans asked what they had to do, he told them, "Don't exact more taxes than is your due." And he said to the soldiers, "Be content with your wages." He pressed home the moral problems that the people faced each day. It was not a message concerning the future but a message concerning their own sinfulness. That was the first part of the prophet's ministry. He addressed a message to his own day in order to bring God's message to that generation.

But, as another part of the prophet's ministry, he often did predict things that would come to pass in the future. An illustration of this is in Jeremiah 25. Notice how specific the prophet was. He was living on the eve of the Babylonian captivity, and he had told the people time after time to prepare for an invasion because God would judge that nation. Then he gave them this word:

> And this whole land shall be a desolation, and an astonishment; and these nations shall serve the king of Babylon seventy years. And it shall come to pass, when seventy years are accomplished, that I will punish the king of Babylon,

> and that nation, saith the Lord, for their iniquity, and the land of the Chaldeans, and will make it perpetual desolations (Jer 25:11-12).

Notice how exact and specific the prophet's message was when he spoke about future things. He said God would bring an invader into Jerusalem who would destroy the city and then carry the people away captive. Seventy years later, that foreign nation would be overthrown, and the people would be permitted to return to their land again. He was so specific that if his message were not fulfilled exactly as it was spoken, then he would be proved a lying prophet, and the God who gave him the message would be a liar. The prophet might also look far down the corridors of time and speak of events that would take place generations in the future. What Jeremiah predicted in 25:11 took place in a matter of months, so the people did not have to wait long to see that prophecy fulfilled. But other prophets were just as specific about events that would not be fulfilled for half a millennium. For instance, the prophet Micah named the insignificant little village where God's Son, the Messiah, would be born (Mic 5:2). How did he put his finger on the birthplace of the Lord Jesus Christ hundreds of years before He came into this earth? Because God knows the end from the beginning. Thus, the prophets delivered a message of condemnation or encouragement to their own people. They spoke of things that were in the near future as well as those in the distant future.

The people might have asked a prophet, "How do we know if what you tell us is of God?" When a prophet delivered a message of condemnation, their own hearts would authenticate the message—their own consciences would bear witness that the message of condemnation was deserved and true. But what about things a year, two years, fifty years or five hundred years hence? There was only one way of telling whether the prophet's message was true. It is referred to in Deuteronomy 18:15. God promised that He would raise up a prophet like unto Moses, God's prophet who had delivered God's message to Israel. The message was so awesome that the people became frightened and asked that God would not speak to them anymore through Moses. They had all that they could take. So God said, "I will not speak further through Moses, but I will raise up a prophet like unto Moses, and he will reveal truth from me." He was speaking of the coming of the Lord Jesus Christ, "the Prophet," referred to so often in the New Testament. But after God promised the Prophet's coming, He gave a test by which to determine whether a prophet is true or false (see vv. 20-22). The principle is very simple. If what a prophet predicts concerning the future comes true, he is a true prophet; but if what he says does not come true, he is false. When Jeremiah prophesied Jerusalem's destruction and the captivity, he was despised and his warning was rejected. He was thrown into a dungeon, and later he was thrown into a well and left to die. But he only had to wait a short time before what he prophesied came true, and the Babylonians came and destroyed the city. Seventy years later Daniel was searching Jeremiah's prophecy when he realized that the end of those seventy years had arrived, and he waited to see what God would do. It was then that God caused a Gentile Persian king to give the Jews permission to go back and rebuild the temple. It demonstrated that the word of the prophet was true. That leads to the first major observation: prophecy was given in God's Word to authenticate a messenger and his message. God had a word for a people, and that word was often so spectacular, so unbelievable, that the people did not or could not or would not accept it. The message might be so awesome and fearful as the message of judgment on Jerusalem, or it might be a blessing such as the promise of the Messiah's coming and they simply could not believe that message could or would be true. So along with that message God gave a definite prophecy so that men through the prophecy's fulfillment might know that the Word of God is true, and that the God of the Word is true. He knows the end from the beginning.

If only the prophecies concerning the first coming of Christ, His birth, His life, and His death on the cross are considered, one has the most staggering demonstration of God's sovereign authority and omniscience. God's Word predicted when Christ would be born, where He would be born, the circumstances of His supernatural birth, the circumstances of His life, the exact details of His death, the fact of His resurrection. All were so minutely spelled out that it would be inconceivable to think of it happening by accident. Someone has figured, using the prophecies of the first coming of Christ, there is only one chance in 87 with 93 zeros after it that the prophecies could be right by chance or by fortuitous guess. Thus, prophecy authenticates God's Word and His message and messengers. Why was prophecy necessary? There was scarcely an Old Testament prophet who delivered a message from God who was not denied by a false prophet. When Moses stood up and delivered the law, there were those who claimed to be prophets and said, "We have as much authority as Moses has. Don't pay any attention to him." And when Jeremiah delivered his message, he ended up in jail. When Ezekiel delivered his message, a multitude of false prophets arose:

> And the word of the LORD came unto me, saying, Son of man, prophesy against the prophets of Israel that prophesy, and say thou unto them that prophesy out of their own hearts, Hear ye the word of the LORD; thus saith the Lord GOD; Woe unto the foolish prophets, that follow their own spirit, and have seen nothing!
>
> They have seen vanity and lying divination, saying, the LORD saith: and the LORD hath not sent them: and they have made others to hope that they would confirm the word.
>
> Because, even because they have seduced my people, saying, Peace; and there was no peace (Eze 13:1, 6, 10).

Jeremiah and Ezekiel had come to the nation and warned that Jerusalem was to be overthrown and that the people would be carried away to captivity. The false prophets stood up and denied the message. What proof did they have?

None, but these false prophets were believed. Why? Because the natural heart will believe what it wants to believe. God not only had to speak about the false prophets, but He had to speak against the false prophetesses. He refers to "the daughters of thy people, which prophesy out of their own heart" (v. 17). These women were soothsayers and diviners who used sacred pillows or handkerchiefs to call up the spirits of the dead. Today they would be called spirit mediums. They were practicing spiritism and were trafficking with spirits of the dead. They said spirits from the dead had told them that what Jeremiah and Ezekiel prophesied was not true. The significant point is, when God had a true message concerning judgment, the need for repentance and forgiveness of sins, then emissaries of the evil one denied the prophet's true word. But the test of the true prophet was whether his prophecy came true. In Genesis 18, three men appeared to Abraham in the plains of Mamre to tell him of two tremendous events that God was going to perform. The first event was that a child would be born to Sarah, who was about eighty years of age, and Abraham, who was nearing one hundred. Another equally spectacular message was that God was about to pour fire and brimstone on the cities of Sodom and Gomorrah and to wipe them out because of their wickedness. Why did God reveal these things to Abraham? The Lord said, "Shall I hide from Abraham that thing which I do?" (18:17). God and Abraham had been walking together in intimate fellowship. Either one of these events would be enough to cause Abraham to doubt unless God took him into His confidence and explained to him ahead of time what He was about to do because He wanted him to be fully aware of His finger in history. We are living today in momentous and significant days. It is that place in time when all the lines of prophecy are converging as trunk lines in a great central terminal. And by knowing God's Word and understanding some of His revelation concerning His program in the world, these movements may be traced.

One such event is the rise of Russia—a momentous thing. Many remember when Russia was insignificant in world affairs. In this generation it has risen from obscurity and impotence in international affairs to a place where it threatens to take over the world. Seldom if ever in the history of the world has a nation arisen with that rapidity and speed. The Word of God tells why it is so significant. Within the last two decades a nation that had no national existence for 2,500 years has been recognized as an independent nation—the state of Israel. Based on the authority of the Word of God, this is one of the most significant events in the last 2,500 years. Why is the little state of Israel so important? The Word supplies the answer. What about the Common Market in Europe and the movement toward refederation? Chapter after chapter in the Old Testament is devoted to that subject and tells of its significance. Those things are all exciting in the light of the Word of God. What about the rise of the political power of the Roman church? Again, chapter after chapter deals with that subject. What about the ecumenical council called in Rome? The Word of God explains its significance. What about lawlessness? Its worldwide progress is traced as part of God's prophetic program. What about the apostasy in the so-called Christian churches, when leaders openly repudiate the virgin birth of Christ and the physical resurrection, the authority and inspiration of the Scriptures? The Word of God tells why that is of significance. God took Abraham aside before He began to unfold this program, and revealed to him what He purposed to do so Abraham could watch it come to pass. That is the second great purpose of prophecy: that the people of God taught in the Word of God might understand the world in which they live and understand the events that are taking place.

Prophecy was designed to bring comfort, hope and assurance to God's people. An example is the famous prophecy of Isaiah 7:14 concerning the virgin birth: "Behold, a virgin shall conceive, and bear a son, and shall call his name Immanuel." The background of the verse is that the king of Syria and the king of Israel, the northern kingdom, had entered into a military alliance. They had agreed to go to Judah and Jerusalem to conquer the little nation, the southern kingdom. Since Judah had no power or resources to resist Syria and Israel, it looked as though she would be destroyed. God sent Isaiah to Ahaz, king of Judah, to tell him that God would remove these enemies. The assurance given to Ahaz was that he could ask a sign which God would fulfill so that he would know that God would remove the enemeis. Ahaz was a wicked, godless king who didn't want anything to do with Jehovah. He knew that if he permitted God to give him a sign that He would remove these enemies, Ahaz would be responsible to submit to Him and obey Him; and he didn't want to do it. Isaiah said he could ask any sign in the heavens, such as to have the sun stand still as He did in Joshua's day, or he could ask anything in the earth beneath, to raise one from the dead as God did in Elijah's day. But Ahaz refused to give God a chance to demonstrate that He was the one to be obeyed. So Isaiah said God Himself would give a sign. And He gave the sign of 7:14, that God would of a virgin produce a son, and that Son would be a deliverer who would deliver Israel from all their enemies. What that prophecy meant to Ahab was that before a young woman could enter into marriage, could conceive and bear a son and then wean that son—a period of about two or three years—this northern coalition would be destroyed and the threat would be averted. What God said to the wicked king Ahaz was this: In two or three years God will turn these people back and they will cease to be a threat. And when you see that happen, you will remember that God is going to send a deliverer. And even though it was more than five hundred years before the deliverer came, God's Word was to be believed. Why? Because in Ahab's day, the Syrians and Israel were turned aside from Judah.

Why did God give this message to the people? So that they

would rest in comfort and assurance. When they heard that this invasion was coming from the north, they would believe God and say, "God has said that they won't enter the city, and God is true. He is to be believed."

Many movements can be traced that bring terror, dread and fear to the hearts of people; but when we know the Word of God, we know how God is going to handle the problem, and that prophecy has the practical result of bringing us into a knowledge of God's program so that we can possess our soul in peace. The author's desire in this series of studies on prophecy is not to excite the reader's fancy, not to try to give answers to perplexing problems that nobody has seen before in the Scriptures. Christians should not be like the Athenians when they gathered on Mars' Hill to hear or to see some new thing, but should give attention to the unfolding of God's prophetic program in order to come to a new assurance of the trustworthiness of the book and the authority of God's Word, that we might rest in the God who could reveal the end and the beginning. We should understand the significance of events taking place around us and be able to relate them to God's program so that our hearts will rest in Him, knowing that He works all things according to the counsel of His own will.

Then, finally, as we realize that we approach the end of the age, this hope of His coming should cause the believer to do what the apostle John said in 1 John 3:3, he "that hath this hope in him purifies himself." If our understanding of the significance of events leads us to the conclusion that we are approaching the latter days, that knowledge ought to purify us. It should energize and activate us in bringing this gospel message to those who do not yet know Jesus Christ as personal Saviour. I do not know any one area of Scripture that can do more for the child of God than a study of prophecy; it authenticates the message and the messenger, it unfolds the program of God, it brings us the comfort and peace of God, and it purifies us as we live in the hope of His coming.

3

PANORAMA OF PROPHECY

Some students of prophecy have been studying prophecy for a long time and are familiar with the program as outlined in the Word of God. Others have not studied the subject before, so terms such as eschatology, rapture, the tribulation, the man of sin, the judgment of nations, Armageddon, and the millennium are unfamiliar. A panorama of prophecy will give a bird's-eye view of the prophetic program as it is unfolded in the Word of God in order to give a perspective of coming events and show them in their relationship to one another.

If you want to make any subject complex and difficult—no matter how simple it really may be—so that you appear to be brilliant, the easiest thing to do is to change common terms to complex terms so that nobody really knows what you are talking about. Some of the prophecy terminology may sound quite complex, but an explanation of it will show how simple the prophetic picture actually is.

When Christ took the disciples apart into the upper room just before His death, He spoke to them not only of His approaching death and of the new relationship which they would sustain to Him when He was in heaven and they were on earth, but He also talked to them about His coming to earth again:

> I go to prepare a place for you. And if I go and prepare a place for you, I will come again, and receive you unto myself; that where I am, there ye may be also (Jn 14:2-3).

Then shortly after Christ's death and resurrection when the disciples were gathered with Him on the Mount of Olives, they watched as He was taken bodily away from them into heaven, and God dispatched messengers to speak to them these words:

> Why stand ye gazing up into heaven? This same Jesus, which is taken up from you into heaven, shall so come in like manner as ye have seen him go into heaven (Ac 1:11).

And the angels who attended the ascension announced to the disciples that Jesus Christ was coming bodily back to earth, and that every eye should see Him, and the one who ascended would be present on earth again. From the time of the Lord's ascension, those who have had the truth of the Word of God have held to Christ's promise that He would return. Generation after generation from the time of the ascension of Christ has lived confidently expecting the fulfillment of what Jesus promised: "I will come again, and receive you unto myself" (Jn 14:3).

The next event in the prophetic program is called the rapture of the church. Today the word *rapture* means joy; it is an emotion that sets the heart aflame and excites the mind and quickens the pulse. But the word *rapture* as used in connection with the prophetic scriptures means "a change, a translation." It literally means "to snatch away," for the Latin word *rapto,* from which the English word *rapture* is derived, means "to snatch away" or "to pluck out."

The promise that He would come and take Christians to Himself is explained in greater detail by the apostle Paul in 2 Thessalonians. The believers in Thessalonica had heard of Christ's promise, and were looking for His coming. They were convinced that Christ would come at anytime, and they were living each day in the light of the promise of His coming. Then an unexpected thing happened: some of those believers died. The other believers in Thessalonica were discouraged and upset, for they had not realized that the Lord would postpone His return until death would remove some from their midst. They had erroneously concluded that those who had died would miss out on the blessing which was in store for believers at Christ's coming for His own. They thought Christ would come to translate, to snatch away, living believers only, which would mean they would be forever separated from their loved ones. So the apostle wrote to remove their ignorance and to explain what would happen at the translation or the rapture of the church (4:13-18). He said the time would come when the Lord would descend from heaven with a shout and the voice of the archangel and the trump of God, and He would appear in the clouds (v. 16).

At this point Christ will not descend to the earth. He will appear in the clouds and, from the clouds, will give an authoritative command, the same kind of command that a general would give to the troops serving under him. When the Lord issues this command from His vantage point in the clouds, first of all, the dead in Christ shall rise out of their graves and begin an ascent into the clouds to meet the Lord. Then, immediately after this resurrection of believers, the Lord will catch up or snatch up those who are alive, and the living and the resurrected dead ones shall meet each other in their ascent, and they shall be joined into one group. These who were the living and the dead will become the resurrected and the translated, or the glorified ones. Some arrive in glory by resurrection and some by a translation, but the apostle says, "We which are alive and remain shall be caught up [snatched up, raptured] together with them in the clouds, to meet the Lord in the air: and so shall we ever be with the Lord" (v. 17).

That is the hope that is given to believers. It is the assurance that we shall meet the Lord in the air, and it matters little whether we go to meet Him by way of resurrection or by way of translation. The process by which we shall come to be with the Lord is insignificant. The important part is that together we shall meet the Lord in the air, and so shall we ever be with the Lord. This "catching up" or rapture is the next prophetic event for which believers are looking and waiting. It is the fulfillment of what Christ promised the disciples when He said, "I go to prepare a place for you, and if I go and prepare a place . . . I will come again, and receive you unto myself."

Two events in the prophetic program await the church after its translation. The first event that takes place in heaven following the rapture is the judgment seat of Christ. This is explained in 2 Corinthians 5:9-12. Every believer who has been translated into the Lord's presence will be examined so that the Lord may give a reward to those who have faithfully discharged their service for Him. It is concerning this that the apostle writes,

> We labour [or make it our ambition], that, whether present or absent, we may be accepted [approved] of him. For we must all appear before the judgment seat of Christ; that every one may receive [for] the things done in his body, according to that he hath done, whether it be good [acceptable] or bad [unacceptable] (2 Co 5:9).

Following the translation of the church, every blood-bought believer from the time of Pentecost to the time of the rapture will be examined in order that the Lord may give a gracious reward to those who have discharged the stewardship entrusted to them.

The second event prophesied concerning the church is the marriage of the Lamb. This is the event following the judgment seat of Christ in which the church, so frequently called the bride in the New Testament, is presented to the Lord Jesus Christ, the Bridegroom. This is referred to in Jude 24:

> Now unto him that is able to keep you from falling, and to present you faultless before the presence of his glory with exceeding joy.

The word translated "to present" is the technical word that was used by the Greeks for the presentation of the bride to the bridegroom. The ceremony was quite simple. The bride and the bridegroom would come into the presence of the father of the groom who had contracted for the marriage, and the bride's father would take his daughter's hand and put it in the hand of the groom's father. Then the father of the groom would put the bride's hand into the hand of the groom. That was the official presentation and at that moment she became his wife. In 2 Corinthians 11:2 Paul says we have been betrothed to Jesus Christ as a chaste virgin to become His bride and, after the church is translated into glory and has been examined to receive rewards for faithful service, the Father will take the bride and present the bride to Jesus Christ and He will possess that bride as His very own. Christians are looking forward to a wedding, and we will not be spectators. We will be participants, for we who have looked forward for so long to that blessed union with Jesus Christ will be presented to Him and will be His possession for the unending ages of eternity. Those two events then transpire in heaven following the church's rapture or translation.

Following the translation of the church, a seven-year tribulation period will unfold on the earth. The prophecy of the seventy weeks in Daniel 9 tells the length of time from Daniel's day to the coming of Christ and also the period of time in which God will pour out judgment on the earth before Christ's second advent. Since this is a detailed prophecy, it is impossible to go into it at this point. But, by way of summary, following the church's rapture, there will unfold a seven-year period known as the tribulation or the time of Jacob's trouble (Jer 30:7). It is the time of wrath or the time of indignation or, to use the Lord's words, there shall be "great tribulation" such as never was and shall never be again. A great portion of the prophetic Scriptures is devoted to describing the events that will unfold on the earth during this seven-year period, and many of these events will be studied in detail. To summarize briefly: after the rapture of the church, the nations of Europe will form a federation and elect one man as their head. This man is referred to in Daniel's prophecy as "the little horn." He is called "the abomination of desolation" by Christ (Mt 24:15). Paul calls him "the man of sin" or "the son of perdition" (2 Th 2:3), and John calls him "the beast" (Rev 13). This individual will emerge on the world scene as an answer to the threat of world domination by Communism, and the European nations which originally emerged from the Roman Empire will federate together under this one head. The first official act of this man will be to attempt to settle the Arab-Israeli dispute. He will make a covenant with the nation of Israel and guarantee to preserve and protect her from her Arab neighbors who will be federated with Russia on the North. Realizing that a Russian-Arab alliance threatens Israel and that any war generated in Israel would threaten the world, this head of the federated states of Europe will guarantee to protect Israel and hope to avert a third world war by putting his power behind Israel. For three and one-half years the world will exist in that cold-war state where the Russian-Arab alliance will wonder if they dare attack Israel, and the western alliance will build up its strength and rattle its rockets to seek to prevent an invasion of Israel by the Russian-Arab alliance.

In the middle of that seven-year period, or three and one-half years after this covenant is spoken, there will be an invasion of Palestine. The center of interest will move to Palestine and Jerusalem, and for three and one-half years—the last three and one half years of this tribulation period—there will be no less than four invasions of Palestine. It will begin, according to Daniel 11, when the Arab nations move into Israel, and those Arab nations will be joined immediately by the second invader, Russia, who will come down from the north. These two coalitions will meet in Jerusalem, destroy the city, and challenge the world to do anything about it (Eze 38). At that moment God will destroy the Russian-Arab alliance the same way He destroyed Sodom and Gomorrah (Eze 38:22). That will leave the land vacant, and the head of the federated states of Europe will move from Europe over into Palestine (Dan 11:45) and announce that he is the world ruler (Rev 13:7). He will be called a god (2 Th 2:4) and become the only god that can be worshiped; for three and one half years he will seek to dominate the world, ruling as king and god on his throne. At the end of the tribulation period, an alliance of nations from the Orient will move across the Euphrates River to contest this European ruler's right to rule the world. A vast army will march from the East to join battle with the European confederation. At that moment the Son of God will invade the earth, destroying the nations gathered in Palestine. During the seven-year tribulation period, God will pour out judgment upon the earth that will make the Egyptian plagues seem insignificant. The book of Revelation describes in detail the awful judgments that shall destroy the vast majority of the earth's population. War, famine, pestilence and death are divine judgments poured out upon the earth because of man's sin of rejecting Christ and submitting to a man as their god.

At the end of that seven-year period, the Son of God shall descend from heaven, and His feet shall stand again on the Mount of Olives (Zec 14:4). He ascended from the Mount of Olives (Ac 1), and He will come back to that mountain. When He comes, those who had been translated into glory and joined to Him will come with Him. Revelation 20 says that all of the saved ones who were in the graves shall be resurrected to live and reign with Him a thousand years. This is the resurrection of all Old Testament and tribulation saints.

Following Christ's second advent there will be a judgment to separate sheep from goats (Mt 25:31-46). This judgment will determine who has accepted and who has rejected Christ as Saviour. All living individuals at the moment of Christ's return will be brought before Him and judged, and He will divide them into two groups—the sheep and the goats. To the goats on His left hand He will say, "Depart from me you wicked into everlasting fire," and to the sheep He will say,

"Come ye blessed of my Father. Inherit the kingdom prepared for you from before the foundation of the earth." The Lord is coming back to earth in order that He might ascend David's throne and reign as King of kings and Lord of lords. He is to be King in Jerusalem. But he cannot reign over unsaved people; He can only reign over saved ones. And so when He returns to earth the second time, He will not only subdue nations and bring them under His authority (Rev 11:15), but He will judge both Israel and the Gentiles and will separate the saved from the unsaved, excluding the unsaved and receiving the saved ones into His kingdom. Revelation 20 says He shall rule on this earth for a thousand years. *Millennium* is a Latin word meaning "thousand." That is why it is used for the thousand-year reign of Christ on earth. It will be His reign over those who have received Him as Saviour and those who in their natural bodies go into this period of time. He will reign as a universal King, ruling from sea to sea and shore to shore. He will remove all lawlessness, sickness and disease, and control any outbreaks of sin. This earth will become a veritable paradise, an Eden, because the Son of God will rule with a rod of iron. During that period, God will show the world through His Son's reign that He is sovereign, that Jesus Christ is King of kings and Lord of lords, and that only He has the right to reign. When Satan rebelled against God, he said in effect, "God does not have a right to reign. I have as much right to reign as He." Satan has been insisting that he has a right to reign ever since the time of his fall, and he will continue to do so until Christ's second coming. At the second advent he will be bound and then chained in a bottomless pit. He will be removed as a tempter from this earth. God will rule through Christ, and He will be acknowledged as King of kings and Lord of lords, and every knee shall bow before Him and every tongue confess that He is Lord so that God the Father might be glorified.

At the end of the thousand-year reign, Satan will be loosed from his prison for a brief season because those who go into the millennium in their natural bodies will beget children and those children will be born on this earth, as you and I were born, with a fallen sin nature and will need to be redeemed, to be saved by faith in Jesus Christ. Many born during the millennium will give only lip service to Christ, will never really receive Him, but because of the stringent rule of the King, they will be afraid to rebel against Him. So, at the end of the millennium, Satan will be loosed so that all those who had given only lip service to Christ might have an opportunity to rebel against Him to show that they have never been born again. When Satan is loosed, he will draw away from Christ and he will be followed by those persons who only professed to serve the King under whose reign they had lived. After that final rebellion, God will judge the earth by fire (2 Pe 3:10). He will set up the great white throne (Rev 20:11-15). At this judgment, all unsaved men of all ages will be brought to hear the sentence of second death pronounced upon them. They will be banished to eternal torment from Christ's presence and, because they rejected the offer of salvation, will be separated from God forever. Then God will create a new heaven and a new earth. This present earth must be judged because it was the stage upon which the drama of sin was unfolded, and Peter says it shall be renovated by fire, and a new heaven and earth will be created. All the redeemed will be brought into this new sphere in order that they might enjoy God's presence forever (1 Pe 3). This is a brief panorama of the prophetic program; its details are expounded in the ensuing chapters. Christ has promised that at any moment He may appear to take us into His presence, and the resurrected and translated ones will be caught up to meet Him in the air. That event is the rapture. Afterward believers will be examined for rewards at the judgment seat of Christ and then presented to Christ as His bride. But while we are undergoing examination and our marriage in glory, the tribulation period will unfold on the earth in which the European nations will federate together. A cold war will continue for three and one-half years, deteriorating into the greatest holocaust the world has ever seen, as multiplied millions of men march and converge upon Jerusalem to be destroyed at Christ's second advent. When His feet touch the Mount of Olives as He promised, Christ will subdue all nations. Then He will remove unbelievers, and set up His kingdom on earth with those living believers who have received Him as personal Saviour. The redeemed will share in the glory of His reign, and this earth shall finally realize its great desire for peace. At the end of this reign, Satan will be given an opportunity to draw off those who rebel against Christ. They will meet Christ as Judge at the great white throne judgment. This will be followed by the creation of the new heavens and new earth wherein dwelleth righteousness where Christians shall enjoy His presence forever. This is the sweeping panorama of prophecy.

4

RAPTURE OF THE CHURCH AND REBUILDING OF THE TEMPLE

One of the last instructions given me by some members of my congregation before we took off for the Middle East a short time ago was the instruction to see if we could see any signs of the rebuilding of the temple. When we returned the first question asked, and one which I have been asked innumerable times, was, "Did you see any signs of the rebuilding of the temple in Jerusalem?" To the consternation of the questioners, my answer was no. We saw no indication of any rebuilding of the temple in Jerusalem, and could uncover no plan for its rebuilding. I knew what the answer would be before we went, because there is only one place where the temple could be rebuilt and that is on the original temple site on Mount Moriah, which site is now occupied by the Muslim mosque. Until Israel finds a way to remove the Muslim mosque, there is no possibility of rebuilding the temple. We did inquire whether Israel wanted to rebuild a temple, and were assured that they did. When asked where it will be rebuilt, they looked at me in utter amazement, for everybody knows the temple has to be rebuilt on its original site. When asked when it would be rebuilt, they only shrugged their shoulders. Because of the frequency with which the question has been asked, this question of the relationship of the rebuilding of the temple to the church's rapture is dealt with here.

In 2 Thessalonians 2:4 is a reference to a temple that the

lawless one or the man of sin will occupy during his earthly reign. This man of sin, the son of perdition,

> opposeth and exalteth himself above all that is called God, or that is worshipped; so that he as God sitteth in the temple of God, shewing himself that he is God.

The teaching that the temple must be rebuilt before the church's rapture can take place is based on this one verse. No other verse of Scripture refers to it, so that entire interpretation is based on this one verse. However, the temple referred to in this verse cannot be built before the rapture and cannot be used or occupied by the lawless one, the head of the federated states of Europe, until at least three and one-half years after the church has been translated. This is important because if the rapture cannot take place until the temple is built, it is utterly pointless to look for the rapture today because, until that temple is built, the rapture cannot take place.

A few basic and cardinal facts of the prophetic program must be remembered. First, the next event in the calendar of events according to the prophetic Word is the rapture or translation of the church. That is the event referred to in John 14:1-3 and 1 Thessalonians 4:13-17 and 2 Corinthians 15:51-52 when Christ, without prior warning or notice, will suddenly appear in the clouds of heaven with a shout, the voice of the archangel and the trump of God. He will call from the graves all the dead in Christ, catch up all living saints who are on the earth and unite them with the resurrected saints. Thus the resurrected saints and the translated living saints will be united into one body of the redeemed, and they shall be taken together into heaven. That is the event to which Christians look forward: the snatching away, the calling out, or the translation of the church.

After a relatively short interval following the church's translation, the head of the federated states of Europe will make a covenant with Israel for seven years (Dan 9:27). This man will be elected to his position (Rev 17:13). Since World War II, Europe has been moving closer and closer to such a federation, and certain political, judicial and economic ties exist today among the signatory nations within the Common Market. Other nations have been seeking entrance into the Common Market and the time will come when these nations represented by the ten toes in Daniel 2 and the ten horns in Daniel 7 will come together in common cause to elect or appoint over themselves one who is called "the beast" (Rev 13:1), "the man of sin," "the son of perdition" or "the lawless one" (2 Th 2). This lawless one will not begin his rule in Palestine; he will rule from Europe. Scripture does not reveal which nation will provide this leader, nor what his European capital will be.

Frequently the question is asked, Will this man of sin be the pope? This idea should be dismissed immediately, for it is impossible. In Revelation 17 this lawless one and the pope are antagonists who are fighting against each other; thus, they cannot be one and the same.

While this lawless one is ruling over the federated European nations, a power will consolidate itself to the north of Palestine. That power, referred to in Ezekiel 38–39 as the king of the north, we identify as Russia. And allied with Russia will be the Arab states of the Middle East (Eze 38). For the first three and one-half years of the seven years of the tribulation period, this lawless one will be ruling in Europe over nations that were once within the Roman Empire. On the other hand, the king of the north will be ruling his domain from that land which is north of Palestine, Russia. So the world in the first half of the tribulation will be divided into two camps—the northern confederacy (Russia and her Arab allies), and the western or European confederacy. During the first three and a half years of the tribulation period, Israel will be in her land, and Palestine will be at peace. It will be in a state of cold war, to use the popular modern term, but the land will be at rest, trusting the covenant made by the head of the Common Market nations to defend them. This then will be the situation at the beginning of the tribulation period. Not until the middle of that period will the covenant which guarantees Israel her own independence in her own land be broken. Then, according to Ezekiel 38—39, Russia and the Arabs will move into Palestine. A description of this invasion is given in Zechariah's prophecy:

> Behold, I will make Jerusalem a cup of trembling unto all the people round about, when they shall be in the siege both against Judah and against Jerusalem. And in that day I will make Jerusalem a burdensome stone for all people: all that burden themselves with it shall be cut in pieces, though all the people of the earth be gathered together against it. Behold, the day of the LORD cometh, and thy spoil shall be divided in the midst of thee. For I will gather all nations against Jerusalem to battle (12:2-3; 14:1).

Note that this gathering against Jersualem will take place in the middle of the tribulation period. When the nations gather together, "the city shall be taken, the houses rifled, and the women ravished; and half of the city shall go forth into captivity, and the residue of the people shall not be cut off from the city. Then shall the LORD go forth, and fight against those nations, as when he fought in the day of battle" (vv. 2-3). The extended passage in Ezekiel 38—39 reveals that also in the middle of that period, Russia will nudge the Arabs to attack Jerusalem. When the Arab forces move against it from the south, Russia will move against it from the north. Ezekiel 39 describes the desolation of the city of Jerusalem described in Zechariah 12 and 14. Thus, for the first half of the tribulation period the Jewish nation will be in charge of Jerusalem and it will be their capital; but, in the middle of that period, the city will be attacked by the Russians and the Arabs and be totally destroyed. Thus, any buildings that might have been built before the tribulation period began or during its first half will be utterly destroyed because Jerusalem will be literally leveled to the ground. That means that any building that will be used during the last half of the period will have to be built after the Lord destroys the Russian and the Arab armies on the plains of Megiddo.

After Jerusalem's destruction, the head of the European confederacy will move into Palestine. During the first half of the tribulation period this head of the western confederacy will have ruled his empire from somewhere in Europe. He will have stayed out of Palestine because it belonged to the Jews, and he had promised to guarantee them their independence in the land. But in the middle of the tribulation period, after Russia and the Arabs have moved in and then been destroyed, the head of the European confederacy will move into Palestine:

> He shall enter also into the glorious land, and many countries shall be overthrown. . . . But he shall have power over the treasures of gold and of silver, and over all the precious things of Egypt: and the Libyans and the Ethiopians shall be at his steps. But tidings out of the east and out of the north shall trouble him: therefore he shall go forth with great fury to destroy, and utterly to make away many. And he shall plant the tabernacles of his palace between the seas in the glorious holy mountain (Dan 11:41-45).

"The glorious holy mountain" is an Old Testament name for Jerusalem. When this occupier moves into Palestine, he will find the land utterly destroyed by the Arab-Russian armies that have marched through it. In order to consolidate the Middle East under his authority and in order to fill the vacuum created by the annihilation of the Russians and Arabs, he will set the tabernacle of his palace between the seas in Jerusalem, or in the glorious holy mountain. He will be setting himself up as a political ruler in the Middle East and the place from which he rules politically will be called a palace because kings use their palaces not only as royal residences, but as the centers of royal administration. So the palace meant the center of a political authority. Revelation 13:5 says this political ruler will move into Palestine forty-two months before the end of the whole prophetic program, or three and a half years before the end of the tribulation period.

> And they worshipped the dragon [that is, Satan] which gave power unto the beast: and they worshipped the beast, saying, Who is like unto the beast? Who is able to make war with him? And there was given unto him a mouth speaking great things and blasphemies; and power was given unto him to continue forty and two months. And he opened his mouth in blasphemy against God, to blaspheme his name, and his tabernacle, and them that dwell in heaven (Rev 13:4-6).

This political leader will set himself up as a religious leader as well. He who claims political authority and sets up a palace also claims religious authority, and so he will set up what is referred to as a temple. The temple was the center of religious worship and life, just as a palace was the center of authority in political life. This one will not set up his temple before the tribulation begins, nor at the beginning of the tribulation period. He will set it up in the middle of the tribulation. Second Thessalonians 2:4 says he "opposeth and exalteth himself above all that is called God, or that is worshipped." Revelation 13:4-5 says he will set himself up as God in the middle of the tribulation period. So, at the middle of the tribulation period, "he as God sitteth in the temple of God, shewing himself that he is God" (2 Th 2:4). Instead of capitalizing the word God in this verse, read it with a small *g*. He as a god "sitteth in the temple of god, shewing himself that he is god." Thus, in the middle of the week, this one will move into his headquarters. His political headquarters is called a palace (Dan 9). His religious headquarters is called a temple. He makes his headquarters the center of both political and religious authority.

In the Old Testament is a record of two temples. The first is Solomon's temple. The second is the temple of Zerrubabel built after the captivity and described in the books of Ezra and Nehemiah. In the New Testament is a third—Herod's temple that was built to take the place of Zerrubabel's temple. It was the temple that Christ knew in the New Testament. In Matthew 24, Christ described the divine judgment upon that temple, saying that stone would not be left upon stone, but the total building would be destroyed. History reveals that temple was destroyed in the year A.D. 70. The next temple mentioned in God's Word is the temple of Ezekiel (chaps. 40–48). It is the temple that will be built by Israel after the tribulation period and after Christ returns to reign the second time. Thus, the Word tells of four temples: Solomon's temple, Zerrubabel's temple, Herod's temple, and the millennial temple to be built after the second advent. Any building that may be built by Israel in the tribulation period will be disowned by God. It would never be called the temple of God because He could not and would not own and use a temple built by those who had rejected and repudiated His Son. The next temple which the Bible mentions that could bear the title "the temple of God" is the temple that will be built after Christ returns to reign. However, the headquarters of the Antichrist, the lawless one, will be called the temple of God because this man will claim to be God. He will erect this headquarters in the middle of the tribulation period as the center of his political-religious system and call it the temple of God, but God will disown it, and He eventually will judge it when Jerusalem is destroyed again at the end of the tribulation period. The time of the erection of this temple is important because if the nation Israel must build a temple before the rapture so that this lawless one can occupy it after the rapture, then there would be no possibility as yet that the Lord Jesus Christ could come at any time. It wouldn't take long to throw up a building, to get some kind of headquarters there today. It wouldn't take long, but it isn't there now. It can't be there until after the destruction of the Dome of the Rock. As long as that mosque stands, no temple will be built. If Christ can't come until after the Dome of the Rock is removed, it may be a long, long time before He comes. This understanding of the biblical program—that this temple does not have to be built before the rapture—affirms that blessed hope that Christ could come without any delay at any moment of time. Believers live in the light of this imminent hope that the Lord Jesus could come at any moment. His coming could be as near as the next heartbeat, because the program has no barriers. While we watch with interest the events as they develop in Israel as they talk about building a temple to be headquarters of world Judaism, yet we know that Christ's coming does not depend on what Israel does about building a temple. John closed the book of Revelation with the promise, "Behold I come quickly," and Christians are the heirs of that promise. Nothing in the prophetic program prevents His coming. He could come today. Thank God for that comforting assurance. The next event in the prophetic program is not the building of a temple, but the coming of Christ.

5

LAWLESSNESS AND THE END TIMES

THE BIBLE paints no rosy picture for the future of humanity apart from Jesus Christ. It recognizes that there is an age-long conflict or warfare, going on from day to day and age to age in which the prince of the powers of the air, the god of this world, opposes the sovereign God in all that He proposes to do. The apostle Paul says,

> But as it is written, Eye hath not seen, nor ear heard, neither have entered into the heart of man, the things which God hath prepared for them that love him. But God hath revealed them unto us by his Spirit: for the Spirit searcheth all things, yea, the deep things of God (2 Co 2:9-10).

And "the deep things of God" are that purpose and program which God has which center in Jesus Christ. The phrase, "deep things of God," refers to all of the treasures of wisdom and knowledge that are hidden in Jesus Christ. But over against the deep things of God there is another system, the deep things of Satan. The apostle John addresses the church of Thyatira: ". . . as many as have not this doctrine, and which have not known the depths of Satan" (Rev 2:24). The word translated "depths" is the same word translated as "deep things" in 1 Corinthians 2:10. When these two passages are put together, two philosophies, two purposes, two aims or two goals are revealed. The one is called the deep things of God; the other is called the deep things of Satan. The deep things of God center in a Person, Jesus Christ; and the deep things of Satan seek to overthrow and defeat the purpose which God has for Christ and the truth of God as it is in Jesus Christ. In every day and in every age, Satan has consistently been working to undermine the truth of God and to substitute his lie, deception and error. God has been seeking to glorify the Lord Jesus Christ, the one whom God has purposed to make King of kings and Lord of lords. Satan has sought to place his puppets in control over the affairs of this earth. The apostle John recognizes this continuing conflict, for he said believers are to test the spirits (1 Jn 4:1). "Spirits" here refers to teachers who come into an assembly of believers to instruct them in what purports to be the Word of God. But John says the believer is not to believe every spirit, but to try or to test the spirits whether they are of God,

> because many false prophets are gone out into the world. Hereby know ye the Spirit of God: every spirit that confesseth that Jesus Christ is come in the flesh is of God: and every spirit that confesseth not that Jesus Christ is come in the flesh is not of God: and this is that spirit of antichrist, whereof ye have heard that it should come; and even now already is it in the world (1 Jn 4:1-3).

John says, "This is that spirit of antichrist." Or, to paraphrase, the apostle is saying, "This doctrine proceeds from one who is opposed to Christ. You have been taught that this false philosophy, this false program should come, but I tell you, it is even now already in the world." At the time when John was writing, about two generations after Christ's death, he said a philosophy was permeating the world, manifesting itself through this world system, that was diametrically opposed to the person of Christ and opposed to the truth as it is in Christ. John was not looking down the corridors of time to say that in the end time there would appear a spirit of lawlessness. He said that spirit was already operating in his day.

The apostle Paul adds to this in 2 Thessalonians where he

speaks of the coming of one whom he calls that "man of sin" and "the son of perdition" (2:3). Another rendering of "the man of sin" would be "the lawless one." This one opposeth and exalteth himself above all that is called God. He is first characterized by his open opposition to God, and then by his elevation above God. He "opposeth and exalteth himself above all that is called God, or that is worshipped; so that he as God sitteth in the temple of God, shewing himself that he is God" (v. 4). Paul reminds them that when he was with them, he told them these things. They had not yet seen this lawless one, Satan's masterpiece of deception. He was not yet personally and physically present, and there was a good reason. God has not permitted Satan to put him in a place of prominence in the world. Verse 6 says, "Ye know what withholdeth," or "ye know the one who restrains," that is, the Holy Spirit, that this lawless one might be revealed in the time that God has designated for him to appear. But "the mystery of iniquity doth already work" (v. 7). While this personification of the deep things of Satan will not appear until the end times, yet Paul says there is a philosophy, a spirit, an attitude, abroad in the world that will continue and increase until this lawless one comes as the consummation of Satan's lawless system. "The mystery of iniquity [lawlessness] doth already work: only he who now letteth [hinders] will let [keep on hindering] until he be taken out of way." One of the ministries of the Holy Spirit is the ministry of restraining Satan in the development of his program. But the apostle says that it is the Spirit's ministry to restrain this manifestation of lawlessness until the God-decreed time for this coming lawless one to be revealed. If you were to capture a skunk and put it in a barrel and clamp on a lid, the skunk would be confined and limited in his activity, but everyone would still know that a skunk was in the barrel. But what a difference if the lid were taken off and that animal were turned loose to go wherever he wanted! Satan and his lawless system are now being confined and limited, and the Holy Spirit is doing the work of restraining; but evidences of this lawless system of Satan are on every hand. Many today feel that the Spirit of God has at least slipped the lid off the barrel a little bit so that even though the skunk might not yet be turned loose, he seems to be having more freedom now than previously. The author firmly believes that God in our generation is letting us see the development of that lawlessness which will consummate after the rapture in the full display of Satan's lawless system.

In 2 Timothy 3 the apostle describes something of the character of the last days in which the church will exist on the earth: "In the last days perilous times shall come" (v. 1). That phrase, "the last days," is significant to a student of prophecy. It always refers to a very brief period of time before the consummation of the age or period being described. "The last days" is used both in reference to God's program for the church and His program for Israel. "The last days" or a similar expression, "the last times," or "the latter day," or "the last day," when used in reference to Israel, refers to the seven years of the tribulation period and more particularly to the last three and a half years of that period, just before Christ's second advent. That is a relatively small period of time in comparison to God's age-long program for Israel. When the phrase "last days," or "last time" or "latter times" is used in reference to the church as it is here, it refers to a period immediately preceding the church's rapture, the appearance of the Son of God in the clouds to summon believers by resurrection and translation into His presence. When the apostle describes events of the last days for the church, he is not describing that which he views as being age-long, but rather that which will particularly characterize society as a whole immediately preceding the rapture.

In verses 2-5, Paul describes some of the conditions that will exist in the world. These are not conditions in the church but are general and broad social conditions. "Men shall be lovers of their own selves." Man is basically and essentially selfish—he looks out for number one, demanding his rights above all else. This characterizes our day.

"Men shall be covetous," he says next. They desire to have what belongs to somebody else. Men are covetous because they are, first of all, essentially selfish. So they may look at another man's material possession, another man's position, another's man job, another man's wife, and they will stop at nothing that prevents their having it.

"Men will be boasters," bragging about their own accomplishments, their accumulated material things, their influence, their power. This is egomania, whether it appears in the political, religious or educational realm; it is a desire to promote self and be appreciated.

They will be "proud," which emphasizes their self-sufficiency and independence. They will not recognize a need for God or any outside help but will be fiercely independent, and self-sufficient.

They will be "blasphemers," setting aside the truth that is in Christ and substituting natural philosophy for divine revelation. They will rebel against all authority. Men will be "disobedient to parents." They will be "unthankful," viewing anything good that comes to them as their just deserts. Men will not pause to thank God for the blessings He has given because they believe that He owes them that. After all, if from the cradle to maturity men have been imbued with the idea that the government owes them a living, it's not difficult to think that God owes them a living too.

Men will be "unholy." This gets down to the very root of the problem: a lack of conformity to God's holiness. They will be "without natural affection," which does not mean that they will not respond to parental love or mother love, or love of husband and wife, but that they will be without the capacity to love. Their sensibilities and their emotions will have been so dulled and degraded by sin that they will not be able to respond to affection, whether it is a love of God for them or the love of a believer loving them with the love of Christ. They will be strangers to love.

They will be "truce-breakers." Their word will mean nothing, and they cannot be trusted to do that which they say they will do. Many political philosophers, who are not revivalists or students of the Scripture, are alarmed at the studied program of deception that issues from men in high places today, saying that we must withhold information from the nation. They have come perilously close to—if they have not slipped over the brink into—what Paul refers to here as a characteristic of the age: being irresponsible with their word.

They are "false accusers" or, to put it plainly, liars. They are incontinent or insatiable in their lusts, and unrestrained in every manifestation of vice. What passes today in the religious realm for the new morality is nothing more than the incontinence of the last days about which the apostle spoke. Isn't this concept of the new morality an amazing thing? It did not originate in Hollywood; it originated in the pulpits as the preachers condoned license, premarital sex, and unfaithfulness in the marriage relationship. And the apostle describes that as a characteristic of the age.

They will be "fierce" or uncontrollable, "despisers of those that are good," hating any righteous man. They will be "traitors"—untrustworthy or unreliable—and "heady"—uncontrollable or headstrong. The picture is of a horse whose mouth has become so calloused that he can no longer feel a bit; and you can pull on the bit in that horse's mouth and he won't respond because he is insensitive to the bit and to the rein. A "highminded" person is determined to have his own way. They are lovers of pleasure more than lovers of God, or pleasure-minded.

These things in verses 2-4 characterize society in the last days before the translation of the church. But all the time that society is in that state, the apostle points out that they will have a form of godliness but deny the power thereof (v. 5). They will have their form of godliness, but will deny that which is a power unto godliness, that is, the person and work of Jesus Christ. Clippings from current newspapers would illustrate every one of the conditions about which Paul speaks. This means that we are fast approaching that time when the Holy Spirit will remove all restraint from lawlessness and from the evil one, and the lawless system of the tribulation period will break upon this earth.

The only thing that prevents that manifestation of lawlessness now is the presence of Christians here on earth. Satan's program is not underdeveloped; his plans are complete and his strategy has been laid. He has had that all mapped out for decades. But that which prevents this manifestation of Satan is the presence of believers who have not yet been translated.

In the last verse of the book of Judges is a significant statement: "In those days there was no king in Israel: every man did that which was right in his own eyes" (21:25). There was no king to curb lawlessness, so the result was anarchy! Men could not live in that state, so they cried out to God for a king who would be strong enough to curb and control lawlessness so they could live without fear. When men are lawless, they need strong discipline and strong authority to curb that lawlessness. When the nation of Israel went into lawlessness, their only recourse was to ask for a king who had sufficient authority to curb that lawlessness which was destroying the land.

In the New Testament, God has a method to control and curb lawlessness in society. In Romans 13, God's program to curb lawlessness is to "let every soul be subject unto the higher powers. For there is no power but of God: the powers that be are ordained of God." Without reading far in this chapter, it becomes obvious that the powers about which he is speaking here are governmental authorities:

> Whosoever therefore resisteth the power, resisteth the ordinance of God: and they that resist shall receive to themselves damnation. For rulers are not a terror to good works,

> but to the evil [evildoer]. Wilt thou then not be afraid of the power? Do that which is good, and thou shalt have praise of the same: for he is the minister of God to thee for good. But if thou do that which is evil, be afraid; for he beareth not the sword in vain: for he [that is, the governor, the president] is a minister of God, a revenger to execute wrath upon him that doeth evil. Wherefore ye must needs be subject, not only for wrath, but also for conscience sake. For for this cause pay ye tribute also: for they are God's ministers, attending continually upon this very thing. Render therefore to all their dues: tribute to whom tribute is due; custom to whom custom; fear to whom fear; honour to whom honour (vv. 2-7).

The apostle is teaching that God has instituted human government as His right arm. In the hand of government, He has put a sword, and the sword is the means to punish a criminal, an evildoer. Government has the responsibility, the God-given responsibility, to curb lawlessness, to punish evildoers, and to reward those who do good. We pay taxes so the government raised up by God to preserve our liberties and rights might be able to perform the function for which it was appointed by God.

What is the picture given in Scripture? As this age comes to its close, government will fail to perform that function for which it was raised up by God, will fail to punish evildoers, and consequently will become ineffectual; anarchy and lawlessness will result.

I am not speaking as a rabble-rouser; I am speaking in the light of the teaching of the Bible. In this generation there has been a transformation in the concept of government and its functions so that governments are no longer performing the functions for which they were raised up by God. Recent decisions of the Supreme Court to protect the rights of the criminal have made it almost impossible to protect the rights of the innocent and the law-abiding. Not only is it serious that the law-breaker goes unpunished, but more important, the groundwork is being laid for lawlessness which will be uncontrollable when the government gives up its function of punishing the evildoer and rewarding the one who does good. Lawlessness must be the inevitable result. There is a scriptural fallacy in this whole concept of protecting the right of the guilty. According to the Old Testament, when a man broke the law, he automatically gave up his own rights. The government fails to realize that when a man violates the law of God and the law of the land, he has surrendered his rights. That's why Scripture says the criminal is to be punished. The course that the government has adopted will inevitably promote lawlessness, crime and rebellion. The attitude of preachers today in this is serious. This is a subtlety of Satan. When Satan wants to promote his program he never paints it for what it is but always whitewashes it so that it appears to be something else; then he gets all the good and the well-intentioned people to climb on his bandwagon, and they don't realize what has happened. Satan is using certain social movements of our day to promote his program of lawlessness. Many religious groups have taken the lead in civil disobedience and in defying the law of the land. Satan has taken something admirable and has caused multitudes to engage in civil disobedience, which is only one step toward lawlessness. He does not care about the causes which produce civil disobedience, but he is concerned about leading this nation into open lawlessness. If the pulpits will lead the pews in civil disobedience, then the door is open to lawlessness. These actions of court and pulpit are taking this nation further down the path of lawlessness in one decade than it has gone in all the years of her history.

This is the same type of anarchy and lawlessness found in Judges. God gave Israel the man Saul to be their king. After the oppression and the taxation that Israel endured under Saul, God took him away and gave them David, the man of His appointment. God in that has given a picture of the prophetic program, for lawlessness will continue and increase as government becomes totally ineffectual to curb lawlessness, and men will cry out for some strong hand to bring authority and law to the nations again. Satan will have his plan ready. One called "the lawless one," who is also called "the beast" in Revelation 13, will be accepted as a world dictator on the proposition that he can do what Saul did in Israel: bring lawlessness under his authority and bring some semblance of order to the earth again. And God will have to remove that satanic imposter as He removed Saul in order that Jesus Christ, the Prince of Peace, can come as King of kings and Lord of lords and subdue all nations to Himself. There will be no peace, no rest, and no stability in government or society until Christ comes to curb lawlessness by removing the lawless one.

This is indeed a dark picture for not one line in the Bible says this process of lawlessness will ever be reversed. There is no hope other than changing the lawlessness of men's hearts by bringing them into subjection to Christ. Men who find Christ as Saviour and are brought into subjection to Him no longer need government to keep them in line; they are lawful because they are related to Him. This national problem will take more than legislation, discipline, and entertainment and activities to curb the lawlessness of young people. It will take the Lord Jesus Christ—the only one who can curb the lawless human heart. Darkness is settling on this earth as lawlessness increases more and more, but before the lawless one exercises his authority over the earth, the Lord Jesus is going to appear in the clouds and take us to Himself, and we will be joined to Him and be with Him forever.

6

APOSTASY AND THE END TIMES

ABUNDANT EVIDENCE on every hand shows that men are departing from the faith. Not only do they doubt the Word; they openly reject it. This phenomenon has never been as prevalent as today. In the period of church history known as the Dark Ages, men were ignorant of the truth; but never was there an age when men openly denied and repudiated the truth. This open, deliberate, willful repudiation of the truth of the Bible is described in Scripture as one of the major characteristics of the last days of the church on earth. Several passages of Scripture tell about false teaching and false teachers and describe the doctrines these apostates will deny.

That there would be false teachers was recognized by all of the New Testament writers. In 1 John 4:1 the apostle exhorts the believers: "Beloved, believe not every spirit, but try the spirits whether they are of God: because many false prophets are gone out into the world." Notice that he is writing to his "beloved," his children in the faith. They have received and known the truth and have been grounded in it by John himself. But to those who have this knowledge of the truth, John gives a warning: "Believe not every spirit." The word *spirit* here refers to a teacher of the Bible. They are called spirits because the God-given teacher will be controlled by the Holy Spirit in his teaching, which will at all points conform to the truth revealed by the Holy Spirit. John recognized that many teachers would come to an assembly of believers to impart knowledge to them. But just because a man claims to be a minister of the gospel does not guarantee that what he says is the gospel. Just because he professes to be a prophet for God, that does not mean that he is sent by God; nor does the fact that he purports to lead men into the truth of God mean that what he speaks is the truth. Therefore, John is really saying, "Do not believe every teacher who comes to you simply because he professes to come from God, but rather try the teachers."

The word *try* means "to put to a test." This is the word that would be used of assaying ore. If someone were to offer you a carload of ore which he claimed had high gold content, you would be a fool if you did not have it assayed before you paid for it. Thus, the apostle says it is necessary for you to test every teacher and his teaching. It is made very clear in other places in the Bible that the test of any man's doctrine is the Word of God. If he goes contrary to "Thus saith the Lord," and "Thus it is written," no matter what his profession, he is a false teacher. But if he presents the truth of God according to the Word of God empowered by the Spirit of God, that man is God-sent. Therefore, John says, "You must put the teachers to the test as to whether they actually do come from God, because many false prophets are gone out into the world." If a teacher comes with academic preparation or with eloquence and oratory it would be easy to conclude that he is evidently from God and all that he says is to be believed. Thus one who sits under that teacher may become lax and indifferent. He will not test the man's pronouncements in the light of the revealed Word of God; and if he does not do that, he may be led astray. Notice that John warns of the coming of false teachers and says every teacher is to have his teaching subjected to the test as to whether it conforms to the standard—the Bible.

Another passage dealing with the advent of these false teachers in 2 Corinthians 11, where Paul says "For such are false apostles, deceitful workers, transforming themselves into the apostles of Christ" (v. 13). These teachers make a profession that is not backed up by reality. They don't stand up to publicly confess that they are denying Bible doctrines because they don't believe them. They are claiming to be Christ's apostles and the word *apostle* means "one who has been sent." So they profess to have Christ's authority and claim that they are His representatives and spokesmen. But, this is a lie, and they are changing themselves into something that they are not. Paul further explains this in verse 14, where he says it is not surprising that these false apostles will change themselves into apostles of Christ, for "Satan himself is transformed into an angel of light." The kingdom of Satan is a kingdom of darkness, and he is the prince of the powers of darkness; and yet, he professes to come with light. He professes to have spiritual illumination to give to men, but his illumination is darkness itself. Satan does not stand before men in order to reveal his true character; he transforms himself into an angel of light. "Therefore it is no great thing if his ministers also be transformed as the ministers of righteousness; whose end shall be according to their works" (v. 15). The apostle says Satan is subtle and clever, and when he comes he will not reveal his true character until men are prepared to receive his diabolical doctrines without question. He will begin by persuading men that he is God's representative and that the truth that he has to present is God's truth, and step by step he will lead men down the path of darkness until they are so blinded that it will be safe for him to take away the mask. He will then step out from behind that guise of light and let men see that he is darkness because they will have ceased to care whatsoever about the truth. Thus Satan will be an imposter, professing to bring men that which he cannot bring—the light of the knowledge of God; and he will lead men little by little down the path of darkness until they have become confirmed in it.

These two passages have to do with the methodology of the false teachers: their deception, hypocrisy, imitation of God's truth and imitation of the Word of God. Several passages speak of the denials made by these false teachers. In the two passages already discussed, John and Paul warned of a danger present in their own day, when Satan's emissaries would seek to darken the minds of men to the truth of the Bible. But 1 Timothy 4 shows the development of false doctrine and false teachers: "The Spirit speaketh expressly, that in the latter times . . ." (v. 1). Notice the phrase *latter times.* These words refer to the brief period of time before the consummation or conclusion of God's program by the appearance of Jesus Christ. When used in reference to the church they refer to the brief period before the translation or the rapture of the church into glory. Paul, in his writing, moves from the danger that surrounded him to that which would be a chief characteristic of the end times. He says, "The Spirit speaketh expressly, that in the latter times some shall depart from the faith." He is not speaking of "the faith" as the faith principle. True, false teachers will try to convince men that they can be saved by their own works, and they thus will leave the faith principle to trust in a works principle.

But that is not what he means by "the faith" here. It refers to the revealed body of divine truth given by the Holy Spirit of God and contained in the Word of God. The Bible was inspired by the Spirit of God, and the Holy Spirit controlled the writers so they were kept from error. Consequently, this book is inerrant and infallible, and every word is inspired. That belief in the Bible characterized men who received the truth down through the ages. But today it is a minority view, and men have departed from the faith. They have repudiated the authority, integrity, and infallibility of the Word of God. Not only do they reject the Bible itself but they despise and hate the doctrines concerning the person and work of Christ revealed therein. "They shall depart from the faith because they give heed to seducing spirits and the doctrines of demons." The seducing spirits in 1 Timothy 4 are the false teachers referred to by the apostle John. These teachers are not only called seducing spirits because they seduce men away from the truth, but their departure from the faith and their denial of the Word of God means that they were controlled by demons. In fact, Paul calls the teachers demons. When a false teacher denies the doctrines of the Word of God, Paul didn't call them intellectuals who were pursuing the truth and haven't quite come to it yet. He didn't call them "brethren" or "well-meaning people"; he called them devils. The apostle was so committed to the truth of the Word of God that he saw any departure from its doctrines as the work of the devil himself. And any man, no matter how cultured, how educated, how oratorical, how respected in the so-called Christion community he may be, if he denies the truths of the Word of God he is called a devil by the Bible. Paul says people will depart from the faith because they give heed to these false teachers and, while they think that they can stand up against their devilish doctrine, the first thing they will know, they will be led down the path of denial.

Frequently people ask, "Should I get out of such and such a church?" It is God's prerogative to tell a man what he should do and when he should do it. While I cannot tell them what to do about membership, I do have to say there is a danger in continuously sitting under a man who professes to be a man of God who does not believe the Word of God and who does not propagate the truths contained therein; for he will begin absorbing false doctrine without realizing it, and will begin to believe what he hears because he has heard it so often. I do not believe that the person who eventually denies the Bible intended to do so when he began. He listened to a false teacher, enjoyed his oratory, and came back the next week and listened again. He was taking steps toward denial. Soon he says, "I used to believe that, but I don't know anymore." Why? Because he constantly gave heed to seducing spirits, false teachers, and the doctrines propagated by these devils.

What about these teachers? Do they know that they are doing wrong? Paul makes it very clear that they do: "They speak lies in hypocrisy." They profess to be ministers of the truth and they are hypocrites in doing so, and a person can't be an unknown hypocrite. To be a hypocrite you have to know that you are doing wrong, and these who stand as representatives of the devil have the Bible to convince them that they are not men of God, and they are standing there as men of God in the so-called church of Jesus Christ, and their being there is an act of hypocrisy. Why will a man who denies the Word of God still stand up as a man of God and sign his name to a marriage certificate as a "minister of the gospel"? It's because he has his conscience seared with a hot iron. When a portion of the body has been burned with a hot iron, it destroys the nerve cells so that part of the body is insensitive to stimulation. When a man stands up to lead people astray, his conscience has become so insensitive that the Spirit of God can no longer speak to him and say, "You're lying. You're deceiving. You're propagating falsehood." Satan is patting him on the back and making him feel good. The women come up and say, "That was a beautiful sermon," and he is foolish enough to believe it. He goes home feeling perfectly satisfied because those who sat in the pew have applauded what he had to say. They are seared and insensitive to the convicting work of the Spirit of God.

Peter adds his testimony to that of Paul:

> But there were false prophets also among the people, even as there shall be false teachers among you, who privily [*secretly*] shall bring in damnable heresies (2 Pe 2:1).

Notice how he speaks of their doctrine as a damnable heresy. He uses such strong terms because there is no life in what they preach, and if a man follows their doctrine, he will be forever damned. The word *damned* isn't a nice word today, and it has dropped out of the modern vocabulary of most people. We like to think of God as a God of love who will not judge anybody. That's a part of the devil's lie. "The soul that sinneth, it shall die," and the one who rejects Jesus Christ is already under condemnation. Yet these men will bring in their heresies that damn men's souls, but they have to do it "privily," or secretly. Pulpits that for generations had proclaimed the gospel of Christ are now being used to propagate denials of the faith of the Word of God. That's the way the devil operates. He secretly brings in his damnable heresies.

What are these heresies? Peter says, "Denying the Lord that bought them, and bring upon themselves swift destruction" (v. 1). Notice the phrase, "denying the Lord that bought them." That is a reference to the denial of the work of Christ.

> Hereby know ye the Spirit of God: Every spirit that confesseth that Jesus Christ is come in the flesh is of God: and every spirit that confesseth not that Jesus Christ is come in the flesh is not of God: and this is that spirit of antichrist, whereof ye have heard that it should come; and even now already is it in the world (1 Jn 4:2-3).

Put these two passages together: 2 Peter 2 and 1 John 4. The denial of doctrine centers in the person and the work of Jesus Christ—two doctrines that Satan hates above everything else. Satan will take away from a man all of the truth of God that he can. And if he can come to a university intellectual and lead that person to deny all of the Bible, he is delighted. But if he comes to a young man who was brought up in the Scriptures and in the church, and insists on believing the Bible, Satan will make his concessions. If Satan has to concede, he will; but one thing that he cannot concede under any circumstances and permit a man to believe is the revealed truth concerning the person and work of Jesus Christ. Man can believe that the Bible is inspired of God and still go to hell. He can believe that Jesus Christ is a good man and a good teacher and that His teachings are profitable, and still go to hell. But a man cannot believe that Jesus Christ, the eternal Son of God, came in the flesh and died for sinners and offers men salvation by faith in Himself, and accept that personally and go to hell. Satan will concede just as much as the man insists on accepting up to the point of the person and work of Christ.

What is the first thing that is left out of the preaching of Satan's emissaries? The person of Christ, the work of Christ, salvation by faith in Jesus Christ. This is apostasy by the teachers who deny the Word of God and its doctrines. They are on every hand—in pulpits throughout the land, in the chairs in our universities and colleges, bringing in damnable heresies.

But there is another kind of apostasy, and that is the kind to which we would be more subject perhaps. Paul tells Timothy to "preach the Word." He is to

> be instant in season, out of season; reprove, rebuke, exhort with all longsuffering and doctrine. For the time will come when they will not endure sound doctrine; but after their own lusts shall they heap to themselves teachers, having itching ears; and they shall turn away their ears from the truth, and shall be turned unto fables (2 Ti 4:2-4).

Notice he is not talking here about a departure on the part of the preacher but about a departure by the congregation. The first apostasy referred to was a denial by the teacher, but here is an apostasy that pervades those who are taught; it is not so much an outward denial of the Bible as it is indifference to God's Word. Paul says, "The time will come when they [the ones who are taught] will not endure sound doctrine; but after their own lusts [or conforming to their own desires] shall they heap to themselves [or choose for themselves] teachers, having itching ears [who will teach what they want to hear, and they will do it because they have itching ears that they want tickled]" (v. 3). The teacher doesn't have itching ears; those who are taught have them.

There is a tendency for the congregation to discount the sovereignty of the Holy Spirit over the preaching of God's Word, and, discounting the Spirit's right to tell the pastor what to preach, they tell him, "You were kind of rough on us today. How about going a little easy next time? There are certain subjects we would rather you not touch on because they affect us. Now if you want to talk about the sins of others, it is acceptable, but don't touch on our sins." When a man of God who stands to teach the Word of God begins to listen to the congregation, he will be led down innumerable blind alleys, and he'll eventually end up on the rubbish heap being useless to God. Every individual has a different note that he likes to have struck, and it takes something different to tickle all these different ears. This is a danger that confronts believers, for there could be things that we particularly enjoy and want to hear to the exclusion of the full truth of the Bible. Some things we would rather not have touched upon because they come so close to our own experience or our own heart. To turn away from God's Word because it reproves or rebukes or exhorts us to godliness and holiness is a form of apostasy, and multitudes of men, without realizing it, have become Satan's emissaries because they have listened to what the congregation says they want, with their eye on ecclesiastical endorsement and advancement. They are silent on the truths of Bible lest they be cast aside by the heirarchy and, as a result, they have withheld the full counsel of God. When Paul left Ephesus he could say to them, "I have not shunned to declare unto you all [the whole] counsel of God" (Ac 20:27). I do not want to stand before the judgment seat of Christ and have the one who put me into the ministry say that I was false to that privilege and responsibility because I tried to please people in my preaching and neglected the full counsel of God. God grant that we who hold so wholly and completely to the revealed word of truth should fall heir to this kind of apostasy so prevalent today that we neglect the truth that is presented because it is displeasing to us.

The apostle John, in writing letters to the seven churches in the book of Revelation, describes the condition of the professing church in the last days. He wrote to the church of Laodicea, and incidentally, Laodicea means "the people speaking." This is 2 Timothy 4:3 in action. They evidently had a pastor who listened to what they wanted and tried to satisfy them in his preaching, with the result that they weren't built up in the faith, nor were they strengthened in the Lord. They weren't taught the Word of God. The Lord had to say,

> I know thy works, that thou art neither cold nor hot: I would thou wert cold or hot. So then because thou art lukewarm, and neither cold nor hot, I will spue thee out of my mouth (Rev 3:15-16).

To be lukewarm is to be just halfway between. It is trying to be close enough to hot to pass as being hot and close enough to cold to pass as being cold. It becomes all things to all men. When the preacher descends to the level of taking orders from the people of God instead of from the Spirit of God, he will produce nothing but a nauseous mess that God has to cast out. Thus there is apostasy in the teacher's denial and another form of apostasy in the listener's neglect.

It is not necessary to labor the point that today the visible professing church is characterized by unbelieving teachers and ear-tickling members in the congregation. This fact is so prevalent it need not be demonstrated. It is evident that we have progressed in church history to that point where we have a right to expect Christ to come at any moment. Men have become Satan's emissaries, purporting to be angels of light. As a result, those who have sat under their teaching have been led into darkness from which, apart from a sovereign work of God, there can be no recovery today. Nothing in the Bible says that this situation will ever be reversed. I wish that these pulpits that had once proclaimed the gospel could be reclaimed for the preaching of the gospel, but I have never seen it happen. And yet, with the presence of denial, doubt and apostasy on every hand, the hope of Christ's coming shines all the brighter because of the darkness of the apostasy around us. Christians who hold to the truth, who love it and seek to proclaim it, can know that these are the latter days and that the Lord Jesus Christ will come to deliver us out of darkness into His marvelous light. Because of the danger, Christians must put every teacher to the test by seeing if they say, "Thus saith the Lord," and then cleave to the truth. Study the truth, love the truth that you might be found faithful at His coming.

7

WHY THE TRIBULATION?

CHRIST, just before His death, in what is known as the Olivet Discourse, outlined the program of prophetic events for the nation of Israel, from the time of His departure until the time of His coming again. In that discourse are these significant words:

> For then shall be great tribulation, such as was not since the beginning of the world to this time, no, nor ever shall be (Mt 24:21).

Tribulation is used in several senses in Scripture. When Christ was speaking to the disciples in the upper room, He said, "In the world ye shall have tribulation: but be of good cheer; I have overcome the world" (Jn 16:33) He was using the word *tribulation* in the sense of persecutions or trials that come to believers because they belong to Christ, because they are hated by the world for His sake. But in Matthew 24:21, where He refers to the great tribulation, He is using the word in a technical rather than a general sense. When it is used technically in prophecy, it refers to that seven-year period between the rapture or the translation of the church into glory and Christ's second advent. That period will be a time of darkness, trial, and the wrath of God. It is called the time of Jacob's trouble. It is referred to as the seventieth week of the prophecy of Daniel 9. Many different words are used to describe it, but the Lord, speaking of the character of it, said that it would be "great tribulation"—tribulation that was unprecedented, unmatched and unparalleled in its severity and intensity. Talk of the tribulation is enough to strike dread or terror into the heart of any man who has read Scripture concerning the nature of this seven-year period. Thank God for the hope given in Scripture that before this awful time breaks on the earth, believers will be translated out of this world, away from the experiences of the tribulation period, caught up into the Lord's presence.

Many details of the tribulation period are developed in the ensuing chapters. Many events that are so significant today are only portents of prophetic events that will come to their consummation after the church's translation. It is not possible in one study to speak of all the events of the tribulation period. It will be profitable to begin a study of this area by considering the reason for the tribulation period. Several passages show what an awful time this period of the great tribulation will be. In Revelation 8:7, in connection with one of the judgments that will be poured out by God on the earth, says, "The first angel sounded, and there followed hail and fire mingled with blood, and they were cast upon the earth." Notice the next word: "and the third part of trees was burnt up, and all green grass was burnt up." When the Scripture talks here about trees and grass, it means just what it says—trees and grass. This speaks of a catastrophic judgment from God upon the earth that will affect a large proportion of the earth's surface so that nature, the physical world, shall suffer in this calamitous judgment. And if a third part of the earth is smitten with this great catastrophe, it naturally follows that the inhabitants of that portion of the earth will suffer as the earth suffers. This passage shows that this physical world will experience these awful judgments from God. Revelation says:

> And the number of the army of the horsemen were two hundred thousand thousand. By these three was the third part of men killed, by the fire, and by the smoke, and by the brimstone, which issued out of their mouths (9:16, 18).

According to verse 18, a third of the earth's inhabitants will be destroyed in this one single judgment, and this is only one of many judgments that will be poured out upon the earth during the tribulation period. In Revelation 6:15-17, men

> hid themselves in the dens and in the rocks of the mountains; and said to the mountains and rocks, Fall on us, and hide us from the face of him that sitteth on the throne, and from the wrath of the Lamb: for the great day of his wrath is come; and who shall be able to stand?

The tribulation period will be a time in which God's wrath will be poured out upon the earth; this wrath will be manifested in three series of judgments. The first judgment will be disclosed under the breaking of the seals. Six seals will be broken, revealing six outpourings of God's wrath. The second judgment will be revealed in the seven trumpets that blow—each one an additional manifestation of His wrath. The third series of judgments will be revealed in the six vials or bowls that are emptied out upon the earth—again, each one containing God's wrath. Since in all of these judgments God will be visiting His wrath upon the earth, as a result of this outpouring a large part of the earth's surface will be destroyed and a great proportion of its inhabitants will be annihilated as it experiences the great tribulation about which Christ spoke.

In the first place this earth will receive this divine visitation because of the world's rejection of Jesus Christ as the Saviour. At the beginning of the tribulation period, many of the world's nations will elect a ruler who will set himself up not only as a political ruler but also as a religious ruler. Referred to as "the beast" (Rev 13), he will eventually claim worldwide political power and will set himself up as the one object of worship throughout the world, ruling on his throne as God. The world will worship the beast, and divine judgment will come upon them because they have despised God, rejected His Son, and acknowledged a demon-possessed man as their only king and deity.

In Revelation 3:10, in giving a promise to the church of

Philadelphia, John writes, "because thou hast kept the word of my patience, I also will keep thee from the hour of testing." This is the promise that believers will be removed from the world before the tribulation begins. Notice the next word: ". . . which shall come upon all the world to try them that dwell upon the earth." This phrase, "them that dwell upon the earth," does not refer to the geographical location where people live; it refers to the character of the people. They are worldlings or earthlings—people who conform to the world; in this instance their conformity to the world is evident by the fact that they despise God and worship the beast and the false prophet, who promotes the beast as a god.

John says a period of testing is coming on the world to test the worldlings; and the word translated "try" or "test" is the word which means to put something into a crucible to find out its worth. Gold is assayed to find out how valuable the ore is, and ore cannot be assayed without putting it into the crucible and subjecting it to the test. In order to prove to the worldlings that they have nothing that can sustain and keep them because they have rejected Christ, God will deliver them into this great tribulation where they will undergo God's wrath. Isaiah presents this same fact when he says,

> For, behold, the LORD cometh out of his place to punish the inhabitants of the earth for their iniquity: the earth also shall disclose her blood, and shall no more cover her slain (26:21).

Notice the words: "The LORD [will] . . . punish the inhabitants of the earth for their iniquity." The iniquity that is principally in view here is the iniquity of rejecting Jesus Christ and of acknowledging Satan's masterpiece of deception as God. This is referred to by the apostle Paul:

> And for this cause God shall send them strong delusion, that they should believe a lie: that they all might be damned who believed not the truth, but had pleasure in unrighteousness (2 Th 2:11-12).

God is pouring out His wrath upon godless men that they might partake of the fruits of their unrighteousness. In connection with the beginning of the third series of judgments in which God will pour out His wrath, another passage reads,

> And the first went, and poured out his vial upon the earth; and there fell a noisome and grievous sore upon the men which had the mark of the beast, and upon them which worshipped his image (Rev 16:2).

Notice that this visitation of divine wrath is for those who have rejected Christ and have acknowledged that the beast is king and god. In 15:7 these angels have "seven golden vials full of the wrath of God," and God's wrath is reserved in the tribulation period for those who have rejected Christ, who have believed the lie of the devil, who have worshiped the creature instead of the Creator, who have accepted the offer of the beast to be their God, and have turned their backs upon the altogether lovely one, the only one who has the right to rule. The first reason for this outpouring of God's wrath, then, is the rejection of Christ and the worship of a false messiah.

A second reason is given in Scripture why God will pour out these judgments on the nations. When Moses was sent to Pharaoh with a message that Pharaoh was to let God's people go, Pharaoh raised a theological question and said, "Who is God? Why should I obey Him?" And the plagues which were visited upon Egypt through Moses were object lessons in theology. It was God's way of teaching Pharaoh who He was and why Pharaoh should worship Him. The ten plagues were divine judgments to teach Pharaoh that Jehovah was God and beside Him there was no other. Pharaoh was stubborn and would not learn, and God had to add lesson upon lesson until, through the death of the firstborn, Pharaoh had to acknowledge that God was sovereign when God said to him, "Let my people go." God meant what He said, and He had the power to back it up.

It is as though the same question will be asked during the tribulation period. "Who is God? Why should we obey Him? Why should we bow before Him instead of worshiping the beast and the system set up by the false prophet?" And the hand of God will be manifested in a number of significant events during the tribulation period to prove to the world that He is God and that there is no other. God is jealous for His reputation. When another says that he has authority equal to or greater than God's authority, God always moves in to prove that man a liar. When the beast sits on the throne as God, claiming that he is God, God will be moved to defend His own character and to prove that He is God alone. One of the significant events of the tribulation period will be the destruction of the king of the north, referred to in Ezekiel 38—39 as Gog and Magog. We believe that this is the northern or the Russian confederacy, but notice this significant statement when that whole prophetic program is introduced in Ezekiel 36:

> And ye shall dwell in the land that I gave to your fathers; and ye shall be my people, and I will be your God. Then shall ye remember your own evil ways, and your doings that were not good, and shall loath yourselves in your own sight for your iniquities and for your abominations. Not for your sakes do I this, saith the Lord God, be it known unto you: be ashamed and confounded for your own ways, O house of Israel. Then the heathen that are left round about you shall know that I the Lord build the ruined places, and plant that that was desolate: I the Lord have spoken it, and I will do it. O house of Israel, but for mine holy name's sake, which ye have profaned among the heathen, whither ye went. And I will sanctify my great name, which was profaned among the heathen, which ye have profaned in the midst of them; and the heathen shall know that I am the Lord, saith the Lord God, when I shall be sanctified in you before their eyes (vv. 28, 31-32, 36, 22-23).

In chapters 38—39 the prophet describes a divine judgment

in which God in a moment of time will erase an army of multiplied millions. God will do with this great northern power what He did to judge Sodom and Gomorrah. He will destroy them in an instant. Why will God do it? It is God's object lesson to the nations that worship the beast that the beast is not God. He and He alone is God, and God will bring about a judgment that is so obviously from His hand that the nations will have a clear-cut testimony that the God of heaven is the true God and besides Him there is no other. The same thing is seen again in Revelation when God empties His bowls of wrath upon the earth:

> And men were scorched with great heat, and blasphemed the name of God, which hath power over these plagues: and they repented not to give him glory. And blasphemed the God of heaven because of their pains and their sores, and repented not of their deeds (16:9, 11).

Notice that those upon whom this visitation of wrath comes recognize that this wrath comes from God, and they know that it is God who is judging them. But in spite of that fact, because of their hard and inpenitent heart, they will not turn to God, seek His forgiveness, or receive Christ that they may have life. The second reason then for these divine judgments is to give the world evidence that God is God and besides Him there is no other.

A third reason is given in Scripture why God will visit the earth with a great tribulation. When Christ came at His first advent, He came unto His own and His own received Him not. Christ was not sent to Gentiles; He says of His own ministry that He was sent to the lost sheep of the house of Israel. He came to them as David's Son in order that He might set up David's throne and rule according to God's promises. Christ stood before the nation and told them that He was their Messiah, King, and Saviour, and He asked them to receive Him. But the nation said, "Away with Him. We will not have this man to rule over us." The nation willfully and knowingly rejected Jesus Christ as their Saviour and Sovereign, and the nation so blessed of God must experience chastening by God because of the national sin of rejecting Christ.

We are living in a day of ecumenicity when eyebrows are raised when any one people or nation is charged with guilt concerning Christ's death. The New Testament was written before the modern ecumenical movement, and when Peter in Acts 2–3 preached, he said to the nation Israel, "Ye denied the Holy One and the Just . . . and killed the Prince of life" (3:14-15). And he preached so strongly and so forcefully that they cowered and cringed and acknowledged their guilt and said, "What must we do to escape divine judgment?" They knew they were guilty and Peter knew they were guilty. This does not absolve the Gentiles of their responsibility, but Christ never came to Rome. He came to Jerusalem, and He didn't stand in Rome to offer the Romans salvation. He stood in fulfillment of the promises made to Abraham and Abraham's children and offered Himself to Israel as their salvation, and it was that nation that said, "We will not have this man to rule over us." As a consequence of that rejection, Christ said,

> Behold, your house is left unto you desolate. For I say unto you, Ye shall not see me henceforth, till ye shall say, Blessed is he that cometh in the name of the Lord (Mt 23:38-39).

And in Luke 21:24, He said, "Jerusalem shall be trodden down of the Gentiles, until the times of the Gentiles be fulfilled." It is significant that from the time of Christ's death until the present day, Israel has never had much more than a toehold in the city of Jerusalem. Until recently it has always been in Gentile hands, and it will be in Gentile hands when the Lord Jesus Christ as the Deliverer comes and drives out Gentiles and gives the land back to those to whom God gave it when He made His promise to Abraham. The destruction of Jerusalem and the continual Gentile occupation of Palestine are part of God's judgment upon a people who willfully and knowingly rejected the Saviour who was sent to them. Zechariah the prophet speaks concerning the rejection of Christ, using these words concerning the inhabitants of the land:

> For I will no more pity the inhabitants of the land, saith the LORD: but, lo, I will deliver the men every one into his neighbour's hand, and into the hand of his king: and they shall smite the land, and out of their hand I will not deliver them (11:6).

Further on in this prophecy God speaks of the time when Jerusalem will be invaded and two-thirds of Jerusalem's inhabitants will have to flee out of the land; and of those who stay, the vast majority will be slain. This will be a divine judgment on a guilty people because of their sin of rejecting Christ. The third reason then that Christ will pour out His wrath is to judge the nation for their rejection of Christ.

The fourth reason for the judgments of the tribulation period is God's purpose to redeem a people, a group of believers who will be on the earth at His second coming who will be received into the kingdom which He will establish and over which He will reign for the thousand years of the millennial age. Every believer will be taken out of the world at the moment of the rapture so not one believer will be left on the earth. Seven years later, when Jesus Christ comes back to this earth to reign, He will find multitudes who have turned to Him. First of all, there will be multitudes from among the Gentiles, for in Revelation 7 John sees multitudes from every kindred and tongue and tribe and nation who have washed their robes and made them white in the blood of the Lamb. Those Gentiles will have come to Christ during the tribulation period. During that same period, many from the nation Israel will turn to the Lord. The Old Testament closes with this promise:

> Behold, I will send you Elijah the prophet before the coming of the great and dreadful day of the LORD: and he shall turn the heart of the fathers to the children, and the heart of the children to their fathers, lest I come and smite the earth with a curse (Mal 4:5-6).

The New Testament closes with the promise that God will do a work during the tribulation period that will bring a multitude from among Israel to a saving knowledge of Jesus Christ as He will bring a multitude from among Gentiles to the Lord. What will bring this multitude of both Jews and Gentiles to the fountain filled with blood so that they might wash themselves clean from all their stain and sin? Some have felt that the rapture, the departure of all the saints, will have such an effect on the hearts of men that they will turn to Christ and be saved. That seems reasonable and logical. The only difficulty is that there is nothing in Scripture that seems to support it. But what is observed is the principle that as long as men can get along by themselves, they ignore and neglect God and refuse to turn to Him. Not until the bottom falls out will they realize their own helplessness and turn to God and cry, "God help me." Men who are self-sufficient and complacent will be shaken through these awful judgments until they come to recognize their own helplessness, hopelessness and lostness; and in the desperate circumstances in which they find themselves, they will turn to God and cry unto Him.

Whereas the vast multitudes will cry to the rocks and the mountains and ask them to swallow them up and hide them from the wrath of the Lamb, there will be one here and one there who will turn to God for help in that dark hour. So while God will bring this outpouring of His wrath to judge the nations because of their rejection of Christ, to judge Israel for their rejection of Christ, and to prove to the nations that He is God, yet God in grace will use these very judgments and wrath to redeem a remnant. So when Jesus Christ comes to this earth the second time, believers will be awaiting His coming, praying to God, "Even so, come, Lord Jesus." They will greet Him when He comes with shouts of "Hosanna," crying, "Blessed is the one that cometh in the name of the Lord." God's wrath will be poured out in the tribulation period because of men's response to Christ. He will judge Israel because they rejected Christ. He will judge the nations because they worshiped the beast and refused to worship Christ. He will judge the world because the world says, "We do not need Christ." God will defend the name of His Son by pouring out His wrath upon those who reject Him.

8

DOES THE BIBLE PROPHESY AN ATOMIC WAR?

RECENTLY I SPOKE at a prophetic conference. During the song before I was introduced, the back door of the church opened and a little old lady entered. An usher, because of the lateness of the hour, attempted to direct her to a seat in the rear, but she forcefully shook her head and made her way down to the second row from the pulpit. No one could miss her. She was not very tall, but nearly filled the center aisle as she walked. She seated herself and wriggled her way into the seat to get comfortable, then immediately went to sleep. The first time I knew she had awakened was when I paused for a breath and her "Amen" filled the whole auditorium. I hoped she would go back to sleep. I'm not opposed to a Spirit-produced amen, but an amen to prove that one is awake is something else. This occurred several times during my message. At the close of the service she was the first one to come to speak to me. She said, "You left something out tonight." I wasn't sure how she knew, but I said, "What was that?" She said, "You were talking on the subject of the signs of the time, and you didn't say a word about the atomic war. Evidently you need what I have," and she reached into a pocket and pulled out some well-worn tracts. Handing them to me, she said, "If you will read these you will learn what I am talking about." I thanked her and put them in my pocket. Her idea is one commonly held. The question is often asked, "Will there be an atomic war?" Many passages of Scripture are frequently used by those who advocate such a conflagration before the rapture, or even an atomic war during the tribulation period, and it does seem as though Scripture describes the final conflict in terms that very much sound like an atomic warfare.

Some years ago, just after the first atomic blast in the desert in the West, I was visiting in the home of my brother-in-law. At that time he was completing his doctoral studies at Harvard University in physics and theoretical mathematics, working with problems in atomic physics. After breakfast he handed me the Scriptures and asked if I would lead family devotions. I read this portion:

> But the heavens and the earth, which are now, by the same word are kept in store, reserved unto fire against the day of judgment and perdition of ungodly men.
>
> But the day of the Lord will come as a thief in the night; in the which the heavens shall pass away with a great noise, and the elements shall melt with fervent heat, the earth also and the works that are therein shall be burned up. Seeing then that all these things shall be dissolved, what manner of persons ought ye to be in all holy conversation and godliness (2 Pe 3:7, 10).

At the conclusion of our prayer, my brother-in-law got quite excited and said, "I want to read that again." He took the Bible and read it for himself, and said, "I have worked in the atomic field and done a lot of research. If ever I heard a description of an atomic blast, that is it." He added, "I don't know of what other words could be used to better describe atomic fission than those." Then he asked the inevitable question: "Is the earth going to be destroyed by an atom bomb?"

After examining a few passages of Scripture that describe something of the awful holocaust that is coming during the tribulation period, we will try to deal with the question, "Is the Word of God preparing the world for an atomic blast or an atomic war?"

Isaiah describes the judgments that precede the establishment of Christ's earthly millennial reign:

> The land shall be utterly emptied, and utterly spoiled: for the LORD hath spoken this word. The earth also is defiled under the inhabitants thereof; because they have transgressed the laws, changed the ordinance, broken the everlasting covenant. Therefore hath the curse devoured the earth, and they that dwell therein are desolate: therefore the inhabitants of the earth are burned, and few men left (24: 3, 5).

It is very easy to fit what has been written of Hiroshima or other atomic blasts into this passage where Isaiah speaks of the utter desolation of the earth. He also speaks of the defilement of the earth, and then of the burning of the inhabitants so that few men are left. It would be quite easy to say that the prophet is describing an atomic blast as a judgment on the earth during the tribulation period. Another passage seems to indicate this:

> And the slain of the LORD shall be at that day from one end of the earth even unto the other end of the earth: they shall not be lamented, neither gathered, nor buried; they shall be dung upon the ground (Jer 25:33).

Once again, Jeremiah is describing a judgment that shall be poured out upon the earth, a judgment that precedes the Lord's second advent to establish His kingdom; and He describes it in terms such as might be used of atomic destruction. He speaks of the extent of the devastation as from one end of the earth to the other, so that there will be no gathering of the dead. They shall lie unburied, and it seems to suggest, in the light of our present understanding, that they lie unburied because of the earth's contamination as a result of the atomic blast. In Revelation on several occasions John speaks of the great desolation that will be poured out upon the earth. In describing the series of judgments revealed in the breaking of the seals, he says,

> And I looked, and behold a pale horse: and his name that sat on him was Death, and Hell followed with him. And

> power was given unto them over the fourth part of the earth, to kill with sword, and with hunger, and with death, and with the beasts of the earth (6:8).

This is a movement against the earth's population that will carry away in that judgment one-fourth of the earth's population. This beggars the imagination and goes beyond description.

One might question whether this could be atomic war since it says that these are to be killed with sword and with hunger and death, and by beasts of the earth. Doesn't that automatically eliminate any such thing as an atomic war? Not necessarily. It is a principle in Scripture that a prophet always speaks to his own society in terms of the culture of that society. If he talks about transportation it's always by horse, camel, ass, or by boat, never by airplane. If he speaks of farming, it's always in terms of plowing with an ox and reaping with a sickle. Even when the prophets look forward to Christ's millennial reign, they talk about the reaper overtaking the harvester, using speech that was prevalent in their own day. When they speak of instruments of war in the future, they always speak in terms of their own culture, so that they talk about swords, spears and shields as the battle instruments. Those would represent any instrument which might be developed and used in the future. Since John is speaking in terms of his own culture with its knowledge, he could speak of swords and to him that would be a way of speaking of any weapon that might be developed in the future; so the fact that he does refer to swords here does not mean that one-fourth of the earth's population would have to be destroyed by a physical sword. The sword could represent any instrument of destruction. John speaks of that which Isaiah and Jeremiah prophesied: a destruction of a vast portion of the earth's population by this judgment.

In Revelation 8 is a second series of judgments that will be poured out upon the earth. John says,

> And the second angel sounded, and as it were a great mountain burning with fire was cast into the sea; and the third part of the sea became blood (v. 8).

Some believe the mountain here is a great volcano, and that this volcano is John's picture of an atomic blast; and as a cloud rises up as if out of a mouth of a volcano to spread outward to bring its devastation upon a vast area, so John is using the figure of a great mountain to speak of an atomic blast.

> And the third part of the creatures which were in the sea, and had life, died; and the third part of the ships were destroyed. And the third angel sounded, and there fell a great star from heaven, burning as it were a lamp, and it fell upon the third part of the rivers, and upon the fountains of waters; and the name of the star is called Wormwood: and the third part of the waters became wormwood; and many men died of the waters, because they were made bitter. The number of the army of the horsemen were two hundred thousand: and I heard the number of them. And thus I saw the horses in the vision, and them that sat on them, having breastplates of fire, and of jacinth, and brimstone (8:9-11; 9:16-17).

This has been used frequently as a symbolic description of an atomic tank with armor (breastplate) and atomic cannons (belching fire). Then John goes on:

> By these three was the third part of men killed, by the fire, and by the smoke, and by the brimstone, which issued out of their mouths (9:18).

These passages give a horrendous description of widespread death and destruction. Now the question arises: How is this judgment coming? Some minimize this description and say it is just poetic imagery; that God is speaking here of some destruction that is to bring death in its wake, but certainly in a limited scope or to a narrow area. They confine it perhaps just to the land of Palestine or to some other localized area. But recall what Christ said:

> For then shall be great tribulation, such as was not since the beginning of the world to this time, no, nor ever shall be. And except those days should be shortened, there should no flesh be saved: but for the elect's sake those days shall be shortened (Mt 24:21-22) .

Daniel's prophecy gives the exact period of time that the tribulation will cover as seven years. It is to be divided into two equal sections of three and one half years, or 42 months or 1,290 days each. The Word of God is specific even to the number of days within the tribulation period. What did Christ mean then when He said, "except those days be shortened"? The number cannot be reduced or Scripture would contradict itself since the Word tells us the exact number of days. An alternative reading found in the Greek lexicon for the word translated "shortened" is the English word *terminated* or *cut off*. Christ is saying that the judgments of the tribulation period will be so intense that if that period was not cut off, if it was not terminated and men were allowed to go on in their godless rebellion, the whole race would be wiped off the face of the earth. And so He says God will intervene and bring this period of judgment to an end.

The reason Christ has to terminate it is that He has a purpose for this earth and for men on the earth. He is coming to reign as King of kings and Lord of lords; and if the human race were successful in wiping all men off the face of the earth, no one would be left when He came who would receive Him and over whom He could reign and rule from sea to sea and from shore to shore. So that Christ's purposes for this earth and for the race might be realized on the earth during His reign, it is necessary to preserve a remnant who will be redeemed and will be taken bodily into His earthly kingdom. That is why Christ said those days must be shortened. In its missiles the United States has a weapon that in thirty minutes could send a warhead from this country to any country in Europe, and by the explosion of that one warhead could release more destructive power than in all the bombs dropped in World War II. It is staggering to think of it, and we are confident that Russia has the same capabilities. We would be foolish to believe that men could not bring such widespread devastation and destruction as is described in Revelation upon any portion of the earth that they desire should they decide to do so. We are facing the possibility of nuclear destruction and, should such a nuclear war be released upon the earth, it could have no other result than to wipe man off the face of the earth.

The significant thing to observe when Isaiah, Jeremiah, John and Christ speak of these widespread destructions is that these destructions do not come from men. These judgments come from God, and this fact is my comfort. In Jeremiah 25:33 the prophet says "the slain of the LORD." It will not be the United States that triggers an explosion to destroy this vast area of the earth's population so that the bodies will not be buried but be as dung on the ground. It will not be Russia. The Lord will release that judgment. In Revelation this same point is made in a number of passages. In 6:17, speaking of the very judgments about which we were reading in which the fourth part of the earth was slain in verse 8, John says, "For the great day of his wrath is come." The word *his* in that verse refers to the Lamb. The people will say to the mountains and to the rocks,

> Fall on us, and hide us from the face of him that sitteth on the throne [that is, God the Father almighty], and from the wrath of the Lamb: for the great day of his wrath is come (vv. 16-17).

This destruction comes from the throne and from the one who sits on the throne. Thus it is a divine judgment.

> And the third angel followed them, saying with a loud voice, If any man worship the beast and his image, and receive his mark in his forehead, or in his hand, the same shall drink of the wine of the wrath of God (14:9-10).

Notice it is "the wrath of God" which is to be poured out

without mixture in the cup of His indignation, and he shall be tormented with fire and brimstone in the presence of the holy angels, and in the presence of the Lamb.

> And I saw another sign in heaven, great and marvellous, seven angels having the seven last plagues; for in them is filled up the wrath of God. And one of the four beasts gave unto the seven angels seven golden vials full of the wrath of God, who liveth for ever and ever. And I heard a great voice out of the temple saying to the seven angels, Go your ways, and pour out the vials of the wrath of God upon the earth (15:1, 7; 16:1).

Observe that all these judgments that are so devastating and so widespread are specifically said to be "the wrath of God." They are the judgments of God, released by God, not by man.

In Ezekiel 36 is revealed a program by which God prepares Israel and the Gentile nations for the return of Jesus Christ to this earth for the establishment of the millennium kingdom. The prophet speaks of several significant events that will precede Christ's reign. In chapter 37 he tells of the regathering of Israel to the land of Palestine in the vision of the valley and the dry bones. In chapters 38 and 39, he describes another great work of God—the destruction of Gog and Magog—as preparation for the return and the reign of Christ. Again, "Gog and Magog" refers to Russia and, allied with Russia, the Pan-Arab block that will invade Palestine in the middle of the tribulation period. At that time God will destroy that invader the same way Sodom and Gomorrah were destroyed, by fire, brimstone and hail from heaven. What is the reason for these two great works—the regathering of Israel and the invasion of Palestine by the northern confederacy with the resultant destruction of that power? The prophecy says,

> Therefore say unto the house of Israel, Thus saith the Lord God; I do not this [that is, that I'm about to reveal to you] for your sakes, O house of Israel, but for mine holy

> name's sake, which ye have profaned among the heathen, whither ye went. And I will sanctify my great name, which was profaned among the heathen, which ye have profaned in the midst of them; and the heathen shall know that I am the LORD, saith the Lord GOD, when I shall be sanctified in you before their eyes. Then the heathen that are left round about you shall know that I the LORD build the ruined places, and plant that that was desolate: I the LORD have spoken it, and I will do it. And I will set my glory among the heathen, and all the heathen shall see my judgment that I have executed, and my hand that I have laid upon them. So the house of Israel shall know that I am the LORD their God from that day and forward. And the heathen shall know that the house of Israel went into captivity for their iniquity (36:22, 36; 39:21).

From these passages from Ezekiel 36 and 39 it is evident that what God will do in the tribulation period, He will do to demonstrate His power, to convince Israel and the Gentile nations that He is a sovereign God, and that besides Him there is no other God. It must then be evident that these judgments that some say refer to atomic warfare cannot be atomic warfare at all, because if someone in the Kremlin should push a button and send a warhead that landed somewhere in the United States and destroyed it, God would get no glory. Russia would. Or if, conversely, someone in this country should push a button and release a warhead that would destroy Europe, it would not be God who demonstrated His power and authority and demonstrated that men were responsible to Him and needed to get right with Him. The United States military would receive the honor and the glory. If these judgments are to serve God's purpose, these destructions and devastation cannot come from men. That is why the prophet emphasizes that they will be divine judgments and retributions. God will judge the world for godlessness.

Second, He will judge because the world has worshiped the

head of the federated states of Europe. Third, God will send these judgments to bring men to the end of themselves and to bring them to their knees so that some might cry out unto Him for forgiveness, deliverance and protection. In the light of the fact that God must preserve men from all races to go into His earthly kingdom, and in the light of the fact that nuclear war would certainly destroy the earth and make it an uninhabitable place and wipe man from off the face of the earth, it is concluded that the next war will not be an atomic war, but rather the next conflagration will be a judgment from heaven bringing death and destruction upon the earth. It will not be an earthly atomic war, but rather it will be a judgment from heaven in which God, who created all things and who put power in every atom, will by the Word of His mouth release the power which He has placed in the atom; and the earth will witness just such destruction as men fear when they talk about an atomic war.

A question often asked when these things are discussed is, "Will there be another world war before the rapture?" We would have to say we don't know. But a suggestion is in order. In the light of all the characters that God has put on the stage who will play an important part in the tribulation period, it is difficult to see how the Lord can delay His coming to allow time for another world war with all of the destruction that it would entail. This would necessitate such a great regrouping of events and personages to bring them again to the place where they are right now. A number of significant events will take place during the tribulation period. There will be one world church that will be made up of apostate Protestantism and Romanism. There will be the federated states of Europe or the revived Roman Empire. There will be alignment of nations and the four great world spheres–Russia on the north; the Arab states in the south; the Oriental nations–the kings of the east; and then the western or the European confederacy. The nation Israel will be back in the land in unbelief. A great, political religious system, called "the harlot" in Revelation 17, will exist.

We can now see movements that are already in progress that will develop into just such a picture as the Word of God describes for the tribulation period. We are at that point where the stage manager has put all of his actors in place, and he is waiting for the signal to raise the curtain so that the drama can unfold. There is no major actor, power, or program revealed in the Word of God whose foreshadowing cannot be seen right at the present time. Another world war would mean that this fourfold alignment of nations would dissolve. There would be an entirely different alignment of nations. The states of Europe would be divided again. Israel would be out of the land. The development of the political-religious system would be arrested. The present picture would be completely shattered as though you had completed a puzzle only to have a child come along and throw it up in the air. The parts of the puzzle are all there together now, and if there should be another world conflagration it would mean that puzzle would have to be broken up and the parts scattered and we would have to go through a cycle of rebuilding it again to where we are right now. We cannot say that God might not do that. He could bring us up to a point and then draw back and let us go through another circle. He might, but that is not the way God has worked previously. When God prepared the world for the judgment of the flood, He was very patient. He sent Noah and let him warn the people for one hundred years. But when the time of judgment arrived there was no turning back, and judgment came.

When God determined to send the northern kingdom into Assyria, He sent prophet after prophet to warn them. And when the time was right, and the time of judgment came, judgment fell. It wasn't postponed. When God said through the prophets that Judah, the southern kingdom, would go to Babylon, He brought them to the point of judgment and there was no drawing back. Judgment came. When Christ offered Himself to the nation Israel and they rejected Him, Christ said judgment would come and it would come in their generation. God brought the Romans in the year A.D. 70 and they destroyed Jerusalem and carried the people away captive. There was no drawing back.

It seems as though God has prepared this world for judgment. In spite of the generations of preaching and teaching and warning, men have rejected the message of the Word of God, and it appears that God is bringing them now to the time of judgment. The only thing that prevents the beginning of that judgment is the presence of believers here on the earth now. The time could shortly come when the stage master will push the button and the curtain will go up, and those judgments will begin. Again, it is difficult to see how this world could go through the conflagration of another world war in the light of the preparedness of the world for the prophesied judgments as we can see them on the horizon now. Christ said that until the end there would be wars and rumors of wars, and we can expect the continuation of both cold war and hot war. But in the light of the purpose God has for the earth, we do not see how one can reconcile an atomic war with the prophetic program; so our conclusion is that there will not be atomic war before the rapture.

9

SATAN'S IMITATION OF GOD'S PROGRAM

THE APOSTLE JOHN warned the saints, over whom he had been exercising spiritual oversight, of the danger of false teachers. No assembly of believers had been established which had not been attacked by false doctrine. When men had received God's truth, Satan purposed to choke out the truth that had been sown by sowing error. Thus in chapter 4 of his first epistle, John warned that they should not accept the teaching from any man simply because he claimed to be a teacher from God. They had a responsibility to try the spirits whether they were of God. The word translated "try" means "to put to the test." Any teacher who came to the city of Ephesus where John had been ministering and claimed to be a teacher from God was to have his message tested by the revealed Word. The reason that they were to subject these teachers and their teachings to the test of Scripture was that many false prophets had gone out into the world. Paul's testimony is added to John's, for in 2 Thessalonians 2; Paul tells the believers that the mystery of iniquity (or lawlessness) is already at work. Satan is developing a false system that imitates the program of God at as many points as possible. Satan is no innovater nor inventor; he is an imitator. And when Satan discovers a program of God, he imitates it so subtly and cleverly that men may feel they are following God's program or are holding to His truth when in fact they are following Satan's program and are holding to a lie. In 1 John 4:3 John says that antichrist has come and is already in the world.

A program is at work in the world today which has been in operation since the time of the apostles. John calls it Antichrist. The term *antichrist* is often used to refer to an individual who will appear in the last days during the tribulation period after the rapture of the church from the earth. But John uses the term in speaking of a purpose, a program and a philosophy rather than of a person. He says that antichrist, or Satan's antichrist system, is already at work and will continue to be at work down through the age. There are two possible interpretations of the word *antichrist* on the basis of the original text. The prefix *anti* means "against," and it emphasizes Satan's program to oppose Christ. It also means "in place of" or "instead of," one who comes as a substitute for Christ. Satan not only opposes the program of God; it is also a substitute for God's program.

This is an outline of some of God's program which Satan will imitate during the tribulation. He will offer the world an individual who will come on the world scene not only to oppose God's program but also as a substitute for Christ. So he truly is anti-Christ. He is the one about whom Daniel prophesied (Dan 7) who will unite again the nations that emerged out of the Roman Empire under his authority. He is the one whom Daniel and our Lord refer to as "the abomination that desolates" who will invade and destroy Jerusalem and occupy it. This is the one that the apostle Paul refers to in 2 Thessalonians 2 as "the man of sin" or "the lawless one." He is the one whom John refers to in Revelation 13 as "the beast" out of the sea who will unite the nations that emerged out of the Roman Empire under his authority and set himself up as a world dictator during the tribulation period.

How will Satan seek to do through this individual what God will ultimately perform in the person of Jesus Christ? Satan is seeking to give the world a ruler in place of Christ who also will be in opposition to Christ so that he can rule over the world, instead of Christ. God's purpose is to put His Son on David's throne so that Christ might rule over the earth. Matthew 17 records the transfiguration, a miniature, premature picture of the glory that will belong to Jesus Christ when he reigns as David's Son on David's throne. He is the one whom God purposes to put in dominion over this earth. When Paul describes this satanic imitation, he says Satan's imitator is not the Son of God but the "son of perdition" (2 Th 2:3). When Christ comes to the world's throne He will come with divine authority, for He will reign on David's throne over the millennial kingdom by God's authority. After the resurrection, Christ could say, "All power [authority] is given unto me" (Mt 28:18). God's authority was conferred upon His Son so that He might exercise all of God's authority in His reign. But in Revelation 13:2 the satanic imitator has supranatural authority, but not the authority of God: "The dragon [or Satan, chap. 12] gave him his power, and his seat [or throne], and great authority." This is part of Satan's imitation. Christ comes as God's Son, and the lawless one comes as Satan's son. Christ comes with all the authority and power of God, and Satan confers all the authority of hell upon the son of perdition so that he might rule over this earth.

When Christ returns to earth to reign, He will come as the Prince of Peace. In Isaiah 9:6, one of the names applied to the Messiah was Prince of Peace, which depicted His work for men on the earth. Christ will come to turn all swords into plowshares and spears into pruning hooks. He will come to speak peace to the earth just as He spoke peace to the storm-tossed Sea of Galilee. In response to His word, "Be still," there was a great calm, and it is God's purpose to introduce peace to this earth by sending the Prince of Peace to this earth to speak peace to it. Knowing God's program, when Satan puts his puppet on the world's throne to oppose Christ and to be a substitute for Him, this one will profess to bring peace to the earth. In Revelation 6 is a description of the first series of judgments which God will pour out upon the earth during the tribulation period These judgments are revealed as the seals of a sealed scroll are opened and the contents revealed.

> I heard, as it were the noise of thunder, one of the four beasts saying, Come and see. And I saw, and behold a white horse: and he that sat on him had a bow; and a crown was given unto him: and he went forth conquering, and to conquer (6:1-2).

Some have concluded that because Christ is coming on a white horse in Revelation 19 at the close of the tribulation period that this rider on the white horse in Revelation 6:2 must be Christ. That would mean that He would come twice in the tribulation period, once at the beginning and once at the end. However, this rider on the white horse is the subtle, satanic counterfeit. When Christ's coming is foretold, He is pictured as a victorious general riding on a white horse. So Satan, in imitating God's program to send Christ to this earth as a victorious conqueror, portrays his deceiver as a conqueror. His peace program is described in Daniel 9:27, which says the final Gentile world ruler will make a covenant with the nation Israel which will guarantee Israel her rights in the land of Palestine as well as protection from any outside invader, and will promise to settle the Arab-Israeli dispute by putting all of the authority of this satanic puppet behind Israel to bring peace to the earth. Jesus Christ is God's Prince of Peace, and if the world is to be deluded into believing that this satanic counterpart is the one for whom the world has been waiting, then he must introduce peace on the earth. And so, Satan's imitator will claim to introduce peace, deceiving the world into believing that it does not need Christ but has all it needs in Satan's puppet.

When Christ returns to the earth He will unite all nations under His authority as King of kings and Lord of lords. In Revelation 11:15 this announcement is made in connection with the second advent: "The kingdoms of this world are become the kingdoms of our Lord, and of his Christ; and he shall reign for ever and ever." As a result of divine judgment, the peoples of the earth were divided into nations at the time of man's first organized rebellion against God at the Tower of

Babel. They have continued as separate nations not because that is God's ultimate purpose but because of man's rebellion. God's purpose is to unite all peoples and nations and tongues and tribes under the authority of one Man who will rule as God's delegated Ruler. In Genesis 1:28, at the time of creation, God said, "Let them have dominion." The divided earth is a continuing testimony to God's divine judgment upon men because of their rebellion. His purpose for the nations will be realized when Christ as King will unite them under His authority.

But Satan, knowing that purpose and program of God, will imitate it before Christ comes. In Daniel 7 the prophet said that the fourth empire, the Roman Empire, would rule over Palestine and would be divided into a number of emerging nations. This is revealed in the ten horns of the beast. Those nations would continue for an extended period of time in a divided state until the time would come when, in response to Satan's imitation, the nations that had emerged from the old Roman Empire would unite again. This is described in Revelation 17:13 where the ten kings and their kingdoms, that is, the ten into which the Roman Empire had divided, will "have one mind, and shall give their power and strength unto the beast." That verse says that these nations which continued as independent nations will ultimately refederate and reunite under one head. It is our conviction that the European movement known as the Common Market is the precursor to this movement in which the nations that emerged from the Roman Empire will reunite to form a United States of Europe. They will merge by surrendering independence and autonomy, and they will give their authority to this one individual called *the beast.* This beast, in ruling over these refederated nations, will be imitating on a limited scale what Christ will do for all the earth at His return. Since Satan knows God's purpose, he will present his ruler as a world ruler or dictator to whom the nations will become subservient. When the Son of God comes He will appear as "KING OF

KINGS, AND LORD OF LORDS" (Rev 19:16). That is, He will be the King over all who call themselves kings, and Lord over all who call themselves lords. Thus, He will exercise all of the sovereign authority of God and will rule as King over the earth.

In Psalm 110:4 is God's statement to Christ: "Thou art a priest for ever after the order of Melchizedek." Melchizedek combined two offices in one person in that he was a king and a priest. Christ will reign as King by God's authority, but He will also be Priest before God on behalf of man. Knowing this, Satan will imitate this purpose of God. Revelation 13:11-18 says the beast will associate with an individual called a false prophet— the instigator of a new religious system. This system worships the beast and gives him religious authority. When Christ reigns, He will be the object of worship because He is God on the throne; but in Revelation 13:8, John says about the satanic counterpart, "All that dwell upon the earth shall worship him." God, who offers the Lord Jesus Christ as the Mediator between God and man, will find Satan imitating Him, and Satan will set up a religious system that ignores Christ, His person and His work, and directs men to worship the beast and acknowledge him as the sovereign authority in both the political and the religious realm. Isaiah 7:14 is the great prophecy of the virgin birth: "A virgin shall conceive, and bear a son, and shall call his name Immanuel." *Immanuel* means "God with us." The one to whom the world will look in faith when He comes to earth is God come in the flesh. Note the satanic imitation: he "opposeth and exalteth himself above all that is called God, or that is worshipped; so that he as God sitteth in the temple of God, shewing himself that he is God" (2 Th 2:4). All through the book of Daniel, the prophet describes this individual as one who speaks blasphemous things but he does not indicate what this blasphemy is. Not until 2 Thessalonians is Satan's blasphemy explained. He will say to the world, "I am king." That is blasphemy enough when God has said that Jesus Christ is

King. He further says, "I am mediator between God and man." That is blasphemy because Jesus Christ is the only Mediator between God and man. To that he adds the blasphemous assumption, "I am God. Besides me there is no other." And in order to bolster his claims to deity, Satan gives the false prophet the power to work miracles to prove that this one who sits on the throne and claims to be God actually is deity. That is the extent to which Satan goes.

Satan also imitates God's program as outlined in Matthew 24:31. At the time of the second advent, Christ will send His angels and bring God's elect nation, Israel, back to Palestine. Prophet after prophet in the Old Testament predicted that after Israel's dispersion there would be a great regathering, and that the Messiah would bring them into the land, redeem them, and rule over them there. Because this is a prophecy of such long standing, Satan will imitate it. Daniel 9:27 says that this individual, as his first official act after being elected head of the United States of Europe, will issue a covenant to Jews throughout the world, guaranteeing their preservation, security and rights back in the land. As a result of his decree, multitudes of Israelites will flock to Palestine, believing that this decree is the fulfillment of all that God promised to them through Abraham. But then Israel will say, "We do not need any other God. We need no other Messiah because all that was promised in the Old Testament is fulfilled and this individual has given to us our right in the land and has guaranteed our protection." God promised to preserve Israel even though they would be scattered and dispersed, so this individual will promise to preserve Israel. The Israelites will so trust him that they will dwell in unwalled villages in Palestine (Eze 38:11). They will be at rest and fear no invader because this Antichrist will promise them protection. This is indeed significant because Israel is the people of God, the nation chosen by God to fulfill His purposes for this earth. Jesus Christ came the first time as Israel's Messiah, and He will come the second time as Israel's King.

When Christ comes, He will bring the greatest prosperity that the world has ever seen. Many passages predict this. As the result of Christ's return to the earth, Amos says,

> Behold, the days come, saith the LORD, that the plowman shall overtake the reaper, and the treader of grapes him that soweth seed; and the mountains shall drop sweet wine, and all the hills shall melt. And I will bring again the captivity of my people of Israel, and they shall build the waste cities, and inhabit them; and they shall plant vineyards, and drink the wine thereof; they shall also make gardens, and eat the fruit of them. And I will plant them upon their land, and they shall no more be pulled up out of their land which I have given them, saith the LORD thy God (9:13-15).

That is but one of a multitude of passages which describe the great material prosperity that the Messiah will give to those who are in His kingdom when He reigns. Satan will seek to imitate this by instituting an economic system that structures the economy of the whole earth:

> And he causeth all, both small and great, rich and poor, free and bond, to receive a mark in their right hand, or in their foreheads: And that no man might buy or sell, save he that had the mark, or the name of the beast, or the number of his name (Rev 13:16-17).

These verses teach that, in order to imitate the prosperity that Christ will bring to the earth, the one called "the beast" will regiment the economy of all the nations over whom he will be elected as sovereign. He will so control the economy that no man will be able to buy or sell unless he submits to the authority. This will be his method of providing the prosperity that Jesus Christ will bestow upon the earth. Today, in order to keep the economy stable, the government is regimenting the economy, and the government is rapidly gaining control over economic life. This is only a portent of what the beast will do during the tribulation as he regulates all the economy. The purpose of that regulation will be to persuade the world that they are receiving blessings from a god, and that the prosperity that they enjoy is a divine blessing.

When Christ comes He will come with all the power of God to subdue unrighteousness, to control rebelliousness, to curb lawlessness, and to remove all things that would offend from His Kingdom. This is one point which Satan cannot imitate because Jesus Christ is the Son of righteousness who will rise with healing in His wings. As much as Satan might want to imitate Jesus' righteousness, he cannot possibly do so, because he is the lawless one. He is a rebel, and it is revealed in Scripture that ultimately his system, which has imitated God's program at so many points, will collapse in utter anarchy, rebelliousness and lawlessness. Even though Satan will seek to bring peace, blessing, prosperity, and good government to the earth, his system will collapse because he will use lawless men, and lawlessness will prevail. The world which will look to the lawless one to bring all that God has promised to the earth will be shown at Christ's second coming that although Satan may imitate, he cannot regenerate. While Satan may control, he cannot transform, and it will only be through Christ's advent that the earth can have the righteousness, peace, blessing, prosperity and security that God has promised to those who know and love Him.

There is need in these days as perhaps never before for those who know the Lord Jesus to read and study the Word because it reveals God's purpose and the satanic imitation. If believers are not to be drawn into Satan's program, they must know God's program in order to be able to detect the satanic imitation. This is true in the political, social, intellectual, and religious realms. In every realm in which we move today, Satan is imitating the program of God to make his program appear as much like God's as possible. In 2 Thessalonians 2, God said that if men would reject Jesus Christ, He would send them strong delusion that they should believe the lie, and the lie is that Satan's puppet is God. If we wonder how Satan can be so successful in deceiving men, we find here the answer: If men reject the revelation that God has given, they will be deluded so that they can be deceived into believing that what Satan is doing is the fulfillment of God's purpose. The responsibility that the children of God have is, first of all, to know the Word so that they will know the program of God and be able to detect Satan's counterprogram. There is an added responsibility of telling men who are in error that Jesus Christ is the way, the truth and the life. To those who are lost, He is the way. To those who are deluded, He is the truth. To those who are dead, He is the life. We are face to face with the arch deceiver, the imitator, the beguiler. May we be equipped through the Word to be able to detect his deception. May we snatch those from his grasp who have been deceived by him.

10

HOW LONG WILL ISRAEL HOLD JERUSALEM?

MOSHE DAYAN, following Israel's occupation of Jerusalem in the Six-Day War, made a public announcement that Israel was in Jerusalem and would never leave it again. This announcement might be expected of the commander of a victorious army. But in the light of the Word of God, Dayan is no prophet; for God has taken us into confidence concerning His program for Jerusalem, and has told us with certainty that Israel will leave the land and their beloved city again. Some of the prophecies concerning the city of Jerusalem are outlined here in order that as you watch events unfold you might understand what is taking place. No attempt is made to prophesy what may happen during the immediate situation in Israel; but by knowing certain Bible prophecies, you can watch events unfold and see how they prepare for the fulfillment of God's prophetic program. Many were startled to hear newscasters and news analysts, who gave no indication of knowing the prophetic Scriptures, who, at the time of the Six-Day War, said we were watching the beginning of Armageddon; and who felt that it was significant that Russia should be backing Egypt in an attack against Israel. Men seem to realize instinctively that we are living in most significant days. Let me preface this study by saying that while we do not believe that we have seen the fulfillment of prophecy, we have seen the stage being set for the fulfillment of prophecy. I want to make that distinction very clear because the prophecies about which we refer are prophecies that fall in the tribulation period. God has made no revelation about prophecies concerning Israel and Palestine and Jerusalem that will be fulfilled before the rapture of the church, but He has made numerous prophecies concerning the history of this land and this people and this city in the tribulation period.

The first specific reference in the Scriptures to the city of Jerusalem is found in Joshua 10. At the time of the conquest of the land under Joshua's leadership, Jerusalem was one of the cities in the path of the victorious Israelites as they came into the land. Many believe that there may have been a previous reference to Jerusalem in Genesis 14:18 where Melchizedek is introduced as King of Salem. Some feel that Melchizedek came from that area that afterward was known as Jerusalem. This may be so and this reference would certainly make Jerusalem one of the oldest inhabited cities on the face of the earth. But while we cannot be certain concerning the identity of the city from which Melchizedek came, there can be no doubt that there is a clear reference to the city of Jerusalem in Joshua 10:1-3:

> Now it came to pass, when Adoni-zedec king of Jerusalem had heard how Joshua had taken Ai, and had utterly destroyed it; as he had done to Jericho and her king, so he had done to Ai and her king; and how the inhabitants of Gibeon had made peace with Israel, and were among them; that they feared greatly because Gibeon was a great city, as one of the royal cities, and because it was greater than Ai, and all the men thereof were mighty. Wherefore Adoni-zedec king of Jerusalem sent unto Hoham king of Hebron . . .

inviting these kings to come and help him. Then a little later in the same book, the city referred to in 10:1 as Jerusalem is further identified:

> And the border went up by the valley of the son of Hinnom unto the south side of the Jebusite; the same is Jerusalem: and the border went up to the top of the mountain that lieth before the valley of Hinnom westward, which is at the end of the valley of the giants northward (15:8).

There follows a further description of the boundaries of Jerusalem. The city is located on the top of a hill, surrounded by gulleys or valleys some three to four hundred feet deep on three of the four sides. The only level approach to the city of Jerusalem was from the north; the Kidron Valley and the Valley of Hinnom surrounded the city on three sides. These made it a city that was easily defendable, for an enemy could approach from only the one direction. That is why David, speaking of Jerusalem in the Psalms, said that Jerusalem was "beautiful for situation." A comparatively small group of men could defend the city from attack since it was a natural fortress. It was one of the cities that fell in Joshua's campaign and came under the authority of Israel when they conquered the land. Little is said of the city of Jerusalem until the time of David. Second Samuel 5:5-8 says that David reigned in Hebron over Judah seven years and six months, "and in Jerusalem he reigned thirty and three years over all Israel and Judah." After seven years of David's reign, he moved his capital to the city of Jerusalem. Hebron was in a flat plain about thirty miles south of Jerusalem. It could not be readily defended, and so David chose Jerusalem as his royal city. Verse 6 reports that he made preparation to take the city, and verse 7 reads: "David took the strong hold of Zion: the same is the city of David." Then verse 9 says, "So David dwelt in the fort, and called it the city of David." It was not only the royal city, but also was the center of the religious life of Israel, for the ark that had been in Shiloh, about ten miles northeast of Jerusalem, was brought back and put in the city of Jerusalem:

> So David went and brought up the ark of God from the house of Obed-edom into the city of David with gladness. So David and all the house of Israel brought up the ark of the LORD with shouting, and with the sound of the trumpet. And . . . the ark of the LORD came into the city of David (6:12, 15-16).

So Jerusalem became not only the center of David's reign, that is, the political capital; it also became the religious center where the ark of the covenant was placed by David. It was David's purpose, according to 2 Samuel 7, to build a temple which would be the home of the ark, the dwelling place of God in Jerusalem. But David was not permitted to build the temple, because he had been a man of war. God said that the temple was to be built by Solomon, David's son, who was "the Prince of Peace." In 1 Kings 5–8 is the record of the erection and dedication of the temple in Jerusalem. Jerusalem, from the time of David onward, was the very center of Jewish life and thought. As a political, economic, educational and religious center, all the life of Israel revolved around it. In the course of her history, Israel departed from God, abandoned God's law, turned to idols, forsook the temple as the meeting place between God and man, and turned to heathen idols. As a result of her apostasy, God pronounced a judgment on Judah which was to take form of an invasion and captivity. The invader who came into Jerusalem was Nebuchadnezzar. Jeremiah tells the effects of this invasion:

> Now in the fifth month, in the tenth day of the month, which was the nineteenth year of Nebuchadrezzar king of Babylon, came Nebuzar-adan, captain of the guard, which served the king of Babylon, into Jerusalem, and burned the house of the Lord, and the king's house; and all the houses of Jerusalem, and all the houses of the great men, burned he with fire: And all the army of the Chaldeans, that were with the captain of the guard, brake down all the walls of Jerusalem round about (52:12-13).

Nebuchadnezzar's army had two great objectives: first, to destroy the royal house so they could break Israel's political power; and, second, to destroy Israel's temple—the symbol of her religious life. Nebuchadnezzar destroyed the city and the temple in 586 B.C. Isaiah gives the words of those who beheld this destruction:

> Thy holy cities are a wilderness, Zion is a wilderness, Jerusalem a desolation. Our holy and our beautiful house, where our fathers praised thee, is burned up with fire: and all our pleasant things are laid waste (64:10-11).

God had promised that if the nation persisted in idolatry and unbelief they would be judged by a foreign invader and, when the message of the prophets was rejected, God fulfilled His promise, sending Nebuchadnezzar to destroy the temple and Jerusalem.

After the seventy-year captivity in Babylon, Israel was granted permission to return to the land to rebuild the temple and subsequently to rebuild the city. In Ezra 1—3 and Nehemiah 2 is the record of the restoration of Jerusalem and the temple. Haggai the prophet, who beheld the restoration temple, prophesied concerning that rebuilt temple:

> For thus saith the LORD of hosts; Yet once, it is a little while, and I will shake the heavens, and the earth, and the sea, and the dry land; and I will shake all nations, and the desire of all nations shall come: and I will fill this house with glory, saith the LORD of hosts. The glory of this latter house shall be greater than of the former, saith the LORD of hosts: and in this place will I give peace, saith the LORD of hosts (2:6-7, 9).

The Jews who had come back from Babylon had little material resources. Since few skilled artisans were among them, their temple of the restoration was crude and could not be compared with the splendor of Solomon's edifice. But God sent Haggai with the comforting message that God would do a work in that building that would cause the splendor of Solomon's temple to be forgotten, for He would fill that house with glory and it would be filled with the desire of all nations.

Many believe that "the desire of all nations" should be capitalized as a reference to the coming of the Lord who, at His first advent, appeared in the temple and possessed the temple in the Father's name, purging it from the defilement.

He said, "My house shall be called a house of prayer, but ye have made it a den of thieves." Christ frequented the temple during the days of His earthly sojourn, observing the required feasts, and revealing God to Israel there. Then He offered Himself as Saviour and King. But, the nation turned a deaf ear to Him. Matthew records how the Lord Jesus in a most remarkable way fulfilled a prophecy of Zechariah, for on the day of the so-called triumphal entry, He rode from the Mount of Olives across the Kidron Valley into Jerusalem on a colt. He did this because He was conscious of what Zechariah had prophesied that "thy King cometh unto thee, meek, and sitting upon an ass, and a colt the foal of an ass" (Mt 21:5). Knowing that He was God's Saviour and Messiah, He came into Jerusalem to officially present Himself. He went from the Mount of Olives into the temple, and for the second time in His ministry He claimed that temple in His Father's name, possessing it as one who had authority. Shortly after, the nation cried out, "Away with this man. Crucify Him. We have no king but Caesar. We will not have this man to rule over us." Thus Jerusalem was the scene of the offer of Christ to the nation of Israel, and it was the scene of His rejection by the nation. It was the scene of the trial of Christ and the condemnation of Christ and, just outside the walls of the city, He was crucified as a traitor and blasphemous imposter. Before Christ died, He pronounced this judgment on Jerusalem:

> O Jerusalem, Jerusalem, thou that killest the prophets, and stonest them which are sent unto thee, how often would I have gathered thy children together, even as a hen gathereth her chickens under her wings, and ye would not! Behold [and notice these words], your house is left unto you desolate. For I say unto you, Ye shall not see me henceforth, till ye shall say, Blessed is he that cometh in the name of the Lord (Mt 23:37-39).

"Your house is left unto you desolate" was a prophecy of divine judgment upon Jerusalem and the temple because the nation officially rejected Jesus Christ as God's Saviour and

Deliverer. This is paralleled with the announcement that Christ made in Luke 21:24, where He said that because of their rejection of Him as Saviour and King, "Jerusalem shall be trodden down of the Gentiles, until the times of the Gentiles be fulfilled." This gives the history of Jerusalem from the time that Israel rejected Christ until the time that Jesus Christ will come to this earth the second time and His feet will touch the Mount of Olives as described in Zechariah 14:4. Jerusalem was to go through a judgment and to be destroyed. It was to be ruled over by Gentiles, as Luke puts it so graphically, "Jerusalem shall be trodden down of the Gentiles until the times of the Gentiles be fulfilled."

Titus in the year A.D. 70 brought his Roman legions into Jerusalem, besieged the city, conquered it, and then completely destroyed it. After the destruction of Jerusalem, the Jews used to congregate where the temple had originally stood, and there they prayed for the peace of Jerusalem and for its deliverance from Gentile dominion. In the year 127, fearing a revolt, the Romans said the Jews could not come closer than the old temple wall. That wall came to be known as "the wailing wall." The Jews made annual pilgrimages to that ancient wall that had originally been the boundary of the temple area, and there they mourned and wept over the destruction of Jerusalem. For about 2,000 years the Jews have been going to that wailing wall to pray, as the psalmist said, for the peace of Jerusalem and to implore God to send a Deliverer to break Gentile authority so that they could go into the city and build their temple.

At the conclusion of the Six-Day War, Israeli soldiers, some of them with bared heads, stood in front of the wailing wall, able to say for the first time in generations, "This is now ours." But Christ said, "Jerusalem shall be trodden down of the Gentiles, until the times of the Gentiles be fulfilled (Lk 21:24). So, does Israel's capture of the city of Jerusalem in the Six-Day War mean that the times of the Gentiles have ended? No, it doesn't. In the first place, the times of the

Gentiles will not end officially when Israel captures Jerusalem but when Jesus Christ comes to earth the second time and subjugates all nations to His authority: "The kingdoms of this world are become the kingdoms of our Lord, and of his Christ; and he shall reign for ever and ever (Rev 11:15).

Prophecy makes it very clear that Israel will not be freed from Gentile dominion in the plan of God until they are delivered by Christ. Israel may hold Jerusalem temporarily and then have to retreat, or perhaps they will be given Jerusalem as a result of their conquest to hold it for a season, but prophetic scriptures plainly state that Israel's lease on Jerusalem is temporary. I believe that it is short-lived. I do not know whether pressure will be brought to bear by the nations for Israel to retreat to some former boundary so that Jerusalem passes again to Jordan, or whether Jerusalem will be permitted to remain in the hands of Israel, or whether it will be administered jointly. If Israel is permitted to keep Jerusalem, it will be because the nations permit it, so they are still there by Gentile permission. Thus it could not be said that the times of the Gentiles have ended.

Several scriptures show the part that Jerusalem is to play in the tribulation period, for which God is setting the stage today. For example,

> The burden of the word of the LORD for Israel, saith the LORD, which stretcheth forth the heavens, and layeth the foundation of the earth, and formeth the spirit of man within him (Zec 12:1).

Before God makes this prediction, He reveals His power and authority. He states the fact that He is the Creator not only of the earth but of mankind as well, and the one who created the earth and mankind can do as He wills in the earth and with men. This is what God said He would do:

> Behold, I will make Jerusalem a cup of trembling unto all the people round about, when they shall be in the siege both against Judah and against Jerusalem. And in that day

> I will make Jerusalem a burdensome stone for all people: all that burden themselves with it shall be cut in pieces, though all the people of the earth be gathered together against it (Zec 12:2).

The burdensome stone is the upper millstone. Grain put into the mill experiences the weight of that millstone, which grinds it to flour. General Nasser found it a true word that the one who moves against Jersualem will find that it is a burdensome stone. Jerusalem, then, is the focal point of the final conflict of Armageddon.

> Behold, the day of the LORD cometh, and thy spoil shall be divided in the midst of thee. For I will gather all nations against Jerusalem to battle; and the city shall be taken, and the houses rifled, and the women ravished; and half of the city shall go forth into captivity, and the residue of the people shall not be cut off from the city (Zec 14:1-2).

In the above passages it appears as though Israel is occupying Jerusalem at the time these events take place. It would seem that in these days God has opened the door for the first time in 1,900 years so that Israel could be back in Jerusalem so that these prophecies could be fulfilled. As long as Israel is outside of Jerusalem, the city will not be the focal point of those who are attacking Israel. But God seems to be opening the door to let them go back into the city so that the nations can converge upon the Jews who are in Jerusalem. In a vain attempt to exterminate them, nations will move against Jerusalem, not knowing that God is using Jerusalem to attract the nations together for Armageddon so that God's enemies might be judged through those great military movements so that Jesus Christ might be put on a throne to rule over this earth.

In Daniel 9:27 it says that the head of the United States of Europe will make a covenant with many for one week. The one who makes this covenant is the one referred to in Daniel 7 as "the little horn" or in Revelation 13 as "the beast." He will make a covenant with many, that is, the nation Israel, to guarantee them their rights in the land. On the basis of this, if we are as near to our Lord's coming as I believe we are, it would not be surprising to see the West demand that Israel keep all of the land that they have taken in the Six-Day War. On the other hand, the Arab states, with those nations who back them, will say that Israel can't keep any of it and they must draw back. It will be against such a conflict, as to how much land Israel will actually possess, that the head of the federated states of Europe will make this covenant with Israel for seven years' duration. The fact that the United States of Europe will make a covenant with Israel strongly suggests that they will be in the land. The fact that Jerusalem is the bone of contention indicates that Israel will have Jerusalem and actually be possessing the city. Second Thessalonians 2 and Revelation 13 say that when the king of the north has been destroyed, and the west moves into Palestine, that the king of the west, or the beast, will occupy a temple and set himself up as a god.

There has been much interest recently about the possibility of rebuilding the temple that would be the center of Jewish worship. It is inconceivable that it should be built elsewhere than on the original temple site. The nation Israel would never settle for less. The following is from a large advertisement addressed to persons of the Jewish faith all over the world:

> A project to rebuild the temple of God in Israel is now being started. With divine help and guidance the temple will be completed. It will signal a new era in Judaism. Jews will be inspired to conduct themselves in such a moral way that our Maker will see fit to pay us a visit here on the earth. Imagine the warm feelings that will be ours when this happy event takes place. *This is My God* by Herman Walk is the book that was the inspiration for this undertaking. God will place in the minds of many persons in all walks of Jewish life the desire to participate in this work. Executive talent, administrators, and workers from all levels

> are needed. All efforts will be anonymous. God will know those desiring to participate. Please write to Box M917, the Washington Post. Under no circumstances send contributions. God's will will prevail.*

This was published as a call to world Judaism and to all physical descendants of Abraham to plan for the rebuilding of a temple. Where will it be built? In Jerusalem. Such a temple as this, according to 2 Thessalonians 2 and Revelation 13, will be occupied as the headquarters of the beast when he rules Palestine. God is opening the way and preparing the stage to put these significant things together that prophecy might be fulfilled. Zechariah says that the Jews who are in the land under the covenant with the beast during the tribulation period will be driven out by the invasions that take place.

> And it shall come to pass, that in all the land, saith the LORD, two parts therein shall be cut off and die; but the third shall be left therein. And I will bring the third part through the fire, and will refine them as silver is refined, and will try them as gold is tried: they shall call on my name, and I will hear them: I will say, It is my people: and they shall say, The LORD is my God (Zec 13:8-9).

When these invasions of Palestine take place in the campaign of Armageddon, two-thirds of the Jews who live in Palestine will be destroyed. Their only safety will be in flight. Christ described this when He said,

> And when ye shall see Jerusalem compassed with armies, then know that the desolation thereof is nigh. Then let them which are in Judaea flee to the mountains; and let them which are in the midst of it depart out; and let not them that are in the countries enter thereinto. For these be the days of vengeance, that all things which are written may be fulfilled (Lk 21:20-22).

Christ warned that when they saw Jerusalem and the land attacked by armies, they would know that God had set His pro-

**Washington Post* (May, 1967).

gram in motion and it would not be long before the climax would come that would fulfill all that God had predicted. Ezekiel describes the invasion that will scatter the people from Jerusalem and from the land itself. The king of the north

> shalt come up against my people of Israel, as a cloud to cover the land; it shall be in the latter days, and I will bring thee against my land, that the heathen may know me, when I shall be sanctified in thee, O Gog, before their eyes (Eze 38:16).

Such occupancy of the land and of the city of Jerusalem as Israel now enjoys must be short-lived because God will bring invaders into the land to destroy the land and to kill or expel the inhabitants out of the land so only a small remnant will remain. The United Nations will never settle this issue, nor will Russia and the United States bilaterally, because God has a definite program. There will be no peace for the city of peace, Jerusalem, until the Lord Jesus Christ comes to this earth the second time. Is it not strange that the city which means "founded in peace" has known more invasions and destructions by her enemies than any other city that has existed on the face of the earth? There will be no peace for Jerusalem until that about which the apostle Paul spoke in Romans 11:26 is fulfilled: "So all Israel shall be saved [or delivered from the times of the Gentiles]: as it is written, There shall come out of Sion the Deliverer, and shall turn away ungodliness from Jacob: For this is my covenant unto them, when I shall take away their sins." The prophetic program shows that Israel will be in the land and occupying Jerusalem at the beginning of the tribulation. Since things are moving in that direction today, the inescapable conviction is that God is setting the stage and getting all things in order. The only thing that keeps this whole program from coming rapidly to its conclusion is that God has not yet seen fit to send His Son into the clouds to call His children home. He has stayed further development in order to extend for perhaps just a brief moment the day of grace in which He invites men to trust Jesus Christ for salvation.

Perhaps you recognize God's hand in these events. You know that God is sovereign and ruling and overruling. You have watched as preparations for the fulfillment of prophecy have unfolded before your eyes, but you have not settled the issue of your salvation. You have never accepted Jesus Christ as your personal Saviour. We cannot presume upon God's grace. If you have not received Christ, while there is still time and opportunity, settle the issue. Receive Him in order that when He comes to receive His own, you will be numbered among the blood-washed ones.

11

THE ALIGNMENT OF NATIONS AND CHRIST'S COMING

UNTIL THE TIME of the call of Abraham, God had been dealing with all men without any reference to their geographical or ethnic background. But with the call of Abraham, God made a division between Jew and Gentile. He said to Abraham in Genesis 12:3, "I will bless them that bless thee, and curse him that curseth thee: and in thee shall all families of the earth be blessed." In this promise God indicated that He had a program for Israel as a nation and also a program for Gentile nations, and that there would be blessing or cursing for both groups.

While the vast part of the Old Testament is concerned with the nation Israel, yet there also is a line of revelation concerning God's program for the Gentile nations. Such great themes as the revived Roman Empire, Armageddon, and the judgment on sheep and goats bring into focus the prophecies concerning the Gentiles. The specific program within these prophecies cannot be understood without some idea of God's division of nations.

The four areas into which the Gentile world powers will be divided at the time of the second advent of Christ will be considered, in order to see the significance in movements that are developing today. This cursory study of the fourfold division of Gentile nations will enable you to read your newspaper or news magazine more intelligently and understand some of the things that are taking place. Nations in the Word of God are divided on the basis of their relationship to the nation Israel, and it is impossible to study the prophetic program for the Gentiles without first seeing the relation of these Gentiles to Israel.

For the student of the prophetic scriptures, one of the most significant events in the last two thousand years was the event that took place in 1948 when the United Nations recognized Israel as a separate nation among the nations of the earth. It was significant because God's division of nations at the end times is a division on the basis of their geographical relation to the land of Israel or the land of Palestine. Nations at the end times will be divided into four different areas: north, south, east, and west. Ezekiel 38 has the first division mentioned. This is the intriguing prophecy concerning God's judgment against Gog, the land of Magog (v. 2). Verse 15 says that Gog, who is the ruler, and Magog, the land over which he rules, "shalt come from thy place out of the north parts." On the basis of this verse, this man Gog from the land Magog is often referred to as the king of the north. He is called that because he will move against Palestine from his homeland located north of Palestine.

On the basis of the nations mentioned in Genesis 10, Bible and prophetic students are generally agreed that the land of Magog is the land known today as Russia. Hebrew lexicons identify Magog as the land of Russia. The descendants of Noah following the flood separated to different points of the compass. The Japhethites left Mt. Ararat where the ark rested, which is in present-day Turkey, and traveled northward beyond the Caspian and Black seas and settled in that area known today as the southern part of Russia. Then those tribal people spread out from there, going northward, eastward, and westward, into what is now the central part of Europe. These people have continued from the time of Japheth in that area and will continue until the end times when, according to Ezekiel 38, Russia will bring about a movement of nations against the land of Palestine and will invade that land. While throughout all the Old Testament period, these peoples dwelled in the land, they lived there as an insignificant and unknown people. In New Testament times, even though that land was occupied by these Japhethites, they continued as an unknown people.

Down through history from the time of Christ to the present century, this densely populated area of the earth has been one that had little or no significance in international affairs. It was unknown, unrecognized, and consequently unfeared. And yet, the Word of God says that the final conflagration of nations will begin with an invasion of Palestine from the north. Prophecy anticipated the rise of a great nation, a great world power, from that area of the earth that had been totally unrecognized down through all the centuries of human history. When did Russia begin to emerge as a world power? Here is an amazing thing: a nation that a generation ago was no more advanced physically, educationally or scientifically than it was one thousand years ago has, within one generation, come to the forefront among the nations of the earth. It was inconceivable a generation ago that they would ever dominate such a vast proportion of the earth's surface, and yet the Word of God says that at the end times the first great threat to the security of the nation Israel and the great threat to world peace would not come from the Greeks or the Romans or the other highly educated, artistic people, but from a nation which would emerge out of the north. It was only a little over a generation ago that a few men introduced a system that has spread across the vast proportion of the earth's surface to become the most popular philosophy and ideology in the world today. Thus, the nation Israel has come into existence as a separate nation in your day and mine, and Russia, the king of the north, has risen to the place of world domination.

Daniel has a reference to a second great area into which the nations of the earth will be divided:

> And at the time of the end shall the king of the south

> push at him: and the king of the north shall come against him like a whirlwind (11:40).

The king of the north mentioned here is the same individual named in Ezekiel 38, but in Daniel a second alignment of nations is referred to as being under the "king of the south." This king of the south obviously must be the head of some nation that lies to the south of Palestine because that is the dividing point. Through the Old Testament the nation of Egypt was referred to as "the south" because for more than four hundred years Israel had been in bondage in Egypt. An Israelite in Moses' day knew that the land of the south was Egypt. Through the Old Testament, a reference to "the south" was a reference to Egypt. In Ezekiel 38:7, God said to the leader in Russia, or the king of the north, "Be thou a guard unto them," or as another version reads, "Be thou a commander unto them." This phrase shows that when Russia is ready to invade Palestine, she will have a number of allies under her control. One of these allies, according to Daniel 11:40, is referred to as the king of the south. Some of the other allies over which the king of the north is the commander are given in Ezekiel 38:5-6 as Persia, Ethiopia, Libya, Gomer and Togarmah. There is no difficulty identifying Persia. But the names Ethiopia and Libya are used for two different areas in the Old Testament. On occasion they may refer to African Ethiopia and Libya, or they may refer to some of the area which today is called the Arab states, in the Arabian Peninsula, where Moses fled after he had killed the Egyptian. He married an Ethiopian, one of the daughters of that land. She was one of the Arab peoples, the descendants of Ishmael or Esau dwelling there. Evidently when he refers to Persia, Ethiopia, and Libya (v. 5), the prophet is referring to some of those Arab states who have come from Esau and Ishmael, related to the Jews because of their descent from Abraham, but an unbelieving people. These will be referred to as the Arab states in the present study.

Along with these Arab states, Russia will be a commander

to Gomer and Togarmah (v. 6). Gomer, according to Genesis 10, settled after the flood in the region of central Europe. Togarmah seems to refer to the land around the Caspian and Black seas, or the northern part of Turkey and the southern part of Russia. These names seem to suggest this second great group of nations that will be drawn together—Egypt together with the Arab states and Turkey and that section of the Middle East around the Caspian and the Black seas. For general reference, this will be called the Pan-Arab block in this study; it is referred to as moving under the authority of the king of the south.

How long ago in history did Egypt rise out of the dust of nations to take a significant place in world affairs? Not more than a decade ago. With the rise of Nasser, Egypt emerged out of the darkness that had gripped it. Out of an insignificant place among the nations, she has come to dominate the Middle East. Thus this group of nations has come together under the authority of Egypt, the one called the king of the south in Daniel 11.

But this passage tells another significant thing: the king of the south is not independent and does not act on his own authority. He moves when the king of the north tells him to. What does it mean? If we understand these prophecies aright, it means that the Pan-Arab block will be controlled by Russia and will move only when Russia tells them to do so. All of this took place not hundreds of years ago but in the last few years. Perhaps God is trying to tell us something; for He not only has brought Russia to a place of prominence, but He also is aligning the Arab states under the leadership of Egypt, and Egypt is bringing them over under the leadership of Russia—and all of this is taking place simultaneously.

In Revelation 16:12 is a reference to a third division:

> The sixth angel poured out his vial upon the great river Euphrates: and the water thereof was dried up, that the way of the kings of the east might be prepared.

The king of the east. There is scant reference in the Word of God to this division of world power, but several significant facts are pointed out here. The kings of the east come from lands that are east of the Euphrates River, which was the known world's boundary in Old Testament days. But the prophet speaks of an invasion of Palestine when the kings that will come from beyond the Euphrates will move against the Middle East and catapult the world into yet another conflagration at the end of the tribulation period. Who are these kings of the east? They cannot be identified as can the states in Ezekiel 38 because specific names are not mentioned.

But one very significant movement is taking place today. China has declared herself as independent ideologically from Russia. From the time of Russian domination of China, Russia looked at China as a part of her sphere of influence. The ideology of Russia was superimposed on China, and yet, wonder of wonders, a nation—one about which we know almost nothing today because it is entirely behind the Bamboo Curtain—has revolted against Russia, has declared itself independent of their authority and has launched out on a militancy that even goes beyond the militancy of Red Russia. This division between Russia and China was necessary, Bible students have felt, but they took it by faith. If the kings of the east are to invade Palestine separate from the king of the north, there had to be some division. But not today. For now this rupture is so complete that nations are coming to be so afraid of China that they are looking with kindness even upon Russia. The kings of the east seem to be forming.

The fourth sphere is a coalition of powers that might be referred to as the kings of the west, although Scripture does not call them that. Daniel said four world powers would rule Israel: Babylon, Medo-Persia, Greece and Rome (chaps. 2, 7). He further stated that the Roman Empire in its historical development would fall into division and out of the old Roman Empire there would emerge ten separate nations. This is inferred in the vision of the image with the ten toes or the beast with the ten horns. Those ten toes and ten horns represented the nations that emerged out of the old Roman Empire. Some of those nations are Italy and France, the Low Countries, Spain and Britain. When the Roman Empire dissolved, the power that was once centralized in Rome divided itself out among these emerging member nations, and they have continued in that separate state and will do so until the tribulation period, that brief period just before the Lord's return to this earth in glory. Then those nations will come together and elect one man to become head over them, as described in Revelation 17:13.

What has been the history of Europe since Word War II? Plan after plan, program after program has been designed to do basically one thing—bring Europe together into a united states of Europe. First there were the military alliances, such as NATO, that tied them together. Then there was the Common Market movement that tied them together economically. And within these movements there has been a progression of political union that will eventually see the nations of Europe federating together to form a United States of Europe as the original colonies in this country formed the United States of America. This is a post-World War II development. This is of great significance. The problem in Europe today is the problem of cooperation between these nations that have emerged out of the old Roman Empire and have gone their independent ways for centuries, but now are exploring the ways and means by which they might come together under one head.

Thus, this is the fourth area of political power that is developing in the very direction that prophecy said Gentile nations would move just before Christ's second advent. The king of the north has arisen to try to take over the control of the world. The second great prophesied division, the king of the south, has come into existence, and these fiercely independent peoples have come together in an alliance, the Pan-Arab block, under the leadership of Egypt and are making overtures to Russia to join with them. At the same time, the third great area has come into existence so that a separate power exists in the Orient, the king of the east. In addition, movements in Europe toward federation are discussed in every newspaper and news magazine. All of these programs will come to their fulfillment after the church is translated and believers have been caught up and received unto glory. They will come to their fulfillment in the tribulation period.

But, if in our day we can see the hand of God moving toward the completion of those programs that will be fulfilled in the tribulation, and if the rapture has to take place before the fulfillment of these, who can say that the rapture could not take place right now? One would have to be spiritually blind or grossly ignorant to miss the fact that the hand of God is moving nations, raising up nations that historians said would never rise again, and bringing about alliances of nations and divisions among nations that historians and political scientists have said could never be accomplished. In the last twenty years more has happened in international affairs than has happened for two thousand years, and it has happened according to God's guidebook. God knew what He would do when He foretold what would take place at the end times. Thus God's Word gives the child of God assurance and comfort, and kindles his hope that the time of Christ's coming draws nigh.

12

THE KINGS OF THE EAST

EVENTS TAKING PLACE in the Orient today seem to give one more indication that God is preparing the stage and putting all the actors in place for the final world drama, and is waiting to raise the curtain by the rapture of the church so that these events can take place. To understand the significance of "the kings of the east" or the Oriental powers in prophecy, remember that during the latter days—that brief period between the rapture of the church and the second advent of Christ which is called the tribulation period—the world will be divided into four different political spheres of influence. The first will be under the king of the south, that is, Egypt and the Arab states. The second sphere will be that of the king of the north, or Russia. According to Ezekiel 38, these two spheres are allied together. Russia is spoken of as a commander over the other peoples and nations, and it seems from this passage of Scripture that the Arab states will draw closer and closer to Russia until they are completely under her influence and following her bidding.

The great final world conflagration referred to in Scripture as the campaign of Armageddon will begin in the middle of the tribulation period, that is, three and a half years after the translation of the church into glory, but three and a half years before the second advent of Jesus Christ back to the earth. At that time Russia will suggest to the Arab states that they move into Palestine and capture it. They will urge the Arab states to make this move with the promise that when they move in from the south, Russia simultaneously will move in from the north. They will converge on Jerusalem and overrun the land. This invasion is described in detail in Ezekiel 38. Then Ezekiel 39 says that when these two political powers meet together in Jerusalem to destroy the land and occupy it, God will destroy that political sphere of influence. Those two federations of nations will be destroyed the same way as Sodom and Gomorrah were destroyed in the book of Genesis.

One can readily realize in our present world situation that if Russia and all her allies were suddenly and catastrophically destroyed, a vacuum would result. Evidently when God destroys these two allies (Russia and the Arab states) , the western confederacy (the United States of Europe) will take advantage of the vacuum and move in to occupy the land of Palestine. According to Daniel 11:45, after Russia is removed as a sphere of influence, the head of the European confederacy will move into the region of Jerusalem and set up his headquarters there. Revelation 13:7 says that "the beast," that is, the head of the United States of Europe, will make war with the saints and overcome them.

Notice the next word in verse 7: "Power was given him over all kindreds, and tongues, and nations." This is part of the satanic program of deception, because God from the early chapters of the Old Testament has decreed that He is going to make Jesus Christ the King. Jesus Christ is destined to be King of kings and Lord of lords, and all authority will be given to Him. But Satan will put an imitator on the throne, and Satan's puppet, this one called "the little horn" in Daniel or "the beast" in Revelation, or the "abomination that desolates" in Matthew 24 will become the head of the United States of Europe. As such he will claim worldwide authority. How will it be possible for him to do that in light of the fact that there will be another great sphere of political influence in the latter days, the sphere called in Revelation 16:12 "the kings of the east"? First, it is of great significance that in the days in which we live there should have been a division between Russian Communism and Chinese Communism. According to Ezekiel 38, when God destroys Russia in the middle of the tribulation period, not only will Russia be destroyed and her power broken, but the power of all her allies will be broken as well. Since that is true, if China and the Orient were allied with Russia at the time of the destruction of Russia, the Oriental powers would be wiped out, and it would be impossible for them to revive and become a great antagonist against the authority of this world dictator who is coming.

Although we Bible teachers, in the light of that prophetic picture, expected a break between Russian Communism and Chinese Communism, we were somewhat surprised that it took place before the rapture. Many assumed they would remain as allies until we were in glory, and then that rift would take place. But this rift between the two nations is becoming wider and wider today, until students of international affairs feel there is an irreconcilable gulf between the two.

Another thing to observe is that throughout the Word of God, until Revelation, no reference is made to the Oriental peoples. They had no influence nor effect on Israel in the Old Testament, and no reference was made of them in the New Testament. The missionary journeys that covered the world covered the Roman world, but not the Oriental world, according to the Word of God. Not until the book of Revelation is any mention made of these kings of the east. As far as the biblical world was concerned, the Tigris and Euphrates rivers were the easternmost boundary, and no reference is made to what was beyond the Euphrates River. Yet, those peoples were there, and in God's own time they would have a significant part to play. But the first real reference to them is in Revelation 9 and they are referred to again in chapter 16. Revelation 9 reveals an interesting fact. The apostle John has been describing the great judgments that God will pour out upon the earth during the tribulation. The first series of judgments that will be poured out is described as the breaking of seals, and then there is a second series of judgment pictured as the blowing of trumpets. In 9:13, the sixth angel is blowing on the sixth trumpet. He is describing one of the judgments that God will pour out upon the earth as an evidence of divine wrath. In verse 14, the sixth angel which had the trumpets said, "Loose the four angels which are bound in the great river Euphrates."

Throughout the book of Revelation, angels are used by God as restrainers. They hold things in check so that a program cannot get ahead of its time. God is working according to the strictest timetable and, so that Satan cannot interfere, He has given certain angels the responsibility of thwarting Satan's program and keeping it in check, and not until God permits the restraining angels to remove the restraint can Satan's program develop. Revelation 9:14 says a restraint has been exercised that kept certain peoples or armies beyond the Euphrates River so they couldn't cross it. Scripture does not particularly identify these peoples beyond the great river Euphrates. It simply says they are peoples that come from beyond the Euphrates River, and no further attempt is made to describe them. Therefore, it is impossible to identify them as any specific people to the exclusion of all others, but perhaps this may be a coalition of nations since they are called "kings." They may be identified as Asiatic or Oriental peoples who have been kept out of the sphere of influence that God has given to Israel. God has kept them beyond the Tigris and Euphrates rivers. Verse 15 says, "And the four angels were loosed, which were prepared for an hour, and a day, and a month, and a year, for to slay the third part of men."

God says He will pour a judgment on the earth that will remove one-third of the earth's population from off the earth. This judgment, of such magnitude that it staggers the imagination, is in the form of a marching army. "The number of the army of the horsemen were two hundred thousand thousand, and I heard the number of them." Two hundred thousand thousand is two hundred million. This army is ready to move and bring death and destruction in its wake which will remove one-third of the men. Then, in very figurative language in verses 18-19, the army is described. Since in John's day they didn't have tanks or armored weapons, the most formidable weapon an army could use was an armored horse. John is describing this future army in terms of the most awesome and dreaded piece of military equipment that existed in his day. That is why he describes them as horses prepared for battle. They have breastplates, making them invincible. Their heads are like lions; that is, they can destroy as a lion destroys its prey. "Out of their mouths issued fire and smoke and brimstone." They brought destruction in their wake. One of the most dreaded pieces of military equipment was burning pitch or burning sulphur; and this army brings that kind of destruction. Verse 19 says,

> For their power is in their mouth, and in their tails: for their tails were like unto serpents, and had heads, and with them they do hurt.

He describes the army as a poisonous serpent which can bring death in its wake. This is a very graphic picture of the awesome destruction that this advancing army will spread.

Consider this problem: Beyond the Euphrates is an empire so great, a political sphere of influence so powerful, that it can mass an army of 200 million men. In the light of this existence of this power, how can the head of the United States of Europe claim worldwide power and authority? The problem is, how can this man move his capital to Jerusalem and say, "I am the emperor of the whole world" while there is a sphere of influence strong enough to mass an army of 200 million men? Now either this man trying to rule the world from Jerusalem is a complete idiot or something has happened that to all intents and purposes has nullified the power of this great Oriental confederacy. It may be that this army composed of 200 million men is so occupied with internal affairs instead of external affairs that it can give no attention to anything taking place outside of its own boundary.

A student rushed into my office this last week and said, "Do you have a radio?' I said, "No." And he said, "You didn't hear the broadcast, then?" I said, "No." He was just trembling with excitement. He said, "I heard a broadcast that was relayed by way of Japan from Red China that Mao Tse-Tung had threatened the rebels in his nation with extermination, saying that at his word he could assemble an army of 200 million men to put down the riots." That student had read Revelation 9 before, and no wonder he was so excited.

It seems reasonable to suggest that this large group of men to be slain will not be killed through the march of this army outside of the Orient beyond the Euphrates, but they will be destroyed as this army seeks to put down the revolt and riots within the nations beyond the Euphrates River. They will be so occupied with internal affairs that the head of the United States of Europe, who will set himself up as the world dictator, will feel that the Oriental nations are in such chaos he doesn't have to take them into consideration. After all, Washington operates on just such a basis in dealing with Red China today.

It seems as though John is suggesting in Revelation 9 that one of the great judgments that God will pour out upon the earth will be in the territory of the kings of the east, and that in order to suppress the revolutions and the rebellions against that autocratic power, a third of the earth's population will be destroyed. More than a third of the earth's population exists within the confines of the Oriental nations today, and that 200 million men could conceivably be brought to bear to try to consolidate authority in these Oriental nations and, in consolidating authority, death will be on such a wide scale that the third part of men shall be destroyed. On the basis of what seems to be inferred in this chapter of the Revelation, great significance can be given to the present revolution going on within Communist China, and it is interesting to see the struggle for power there and to follow the steps that the leaders are taking to keep control within the nation. This would answer the question as to how this head of the United States of Europe could proclaim himself a world dictator, and how he could exert authority over the earth without ever being challenged by the Oriental nations who could mass such a great military movement.

Revelation 16 has another brief and yet significant word about the kings of the east. God will pour out a third series of judgments on the earth, and these judgments are symbolized by the emptying of bowls or vials. In the sixth vial, which is the next to the last judgment that God will pour out upon the earth, John says,

> And the sixth angel poured out his vial upon the great river Euphrates; and the water thereof was dried up, that the way of the kings of the east might be prepared (16:12).

This brings us to the very end of the tribulation period. Russia and the Arab states will have been out of the picture for approximately three and a half years. Jerusalem has become the capital of the empire ruled over by the head of the United States of Europe, who has proclaimed himself as both king and god on his throne, and has demanded that all the world worship him. He has instituted such a regimented system that no man can buy or sell unless he has that identifying mark of submission to the beast. But after he rules for three and a half years and is revered by a godless world as their god, God will step in and show the world that this demon-possessed man is not God. All this time the angels will have been keeping the Oriental nations in the Orient. God will suddenly take away that restraint—pictured in Revelation 16:12 as the waters of the Euphrates drying up. When God dried up the Red Sea, the Israelites could leave Egypt on dry land. Forty years later when God dried up the Jordan, the Israelites who had been in the wilderness could march into the land. The drying up of the waters then provided a way of access. God will dry up the Euphrates, that is, provide a way of access, so that the Oriental powers that could mass an army of 200 million to try to suppress revolt within the nation will be able to spill over and begin a march across the fertile crescent toward Palestine. They will come because of their determination to challenge the right of the head of the federated states of Europe who claims worldwide dominion. These two political spheres will prepare for battle, gathering together "into a place called in the Hebrew tongue Armageddon" (v. 16).

Armageddon is the great plain of Esdralon in the north of Palestine that stretches from Mount Carmel forty miles across to the Sea of Galilee. Napoleon marched across it, declaring that it was the world's greatest natural battlefield. It is that battlefield to which God will bring together the armies of the United States of Europe and the armies of the Orient who will be preparing to enter into battle to see who will rule the world. At that time a most significant thing will take place:

> After the tribulation of those days shall the sun be darkened, and the moon shall not give her light, and the stars shall fall from heaven, and the powers of the heavens shall be shaken (Mt 24:29).

Now notice: "And then shall appear the sign of the Son of man in heaven" (v. 30).

The sign that God was present in Israel was the pillar of fire or cloud that reflected God's glory. Israel knew that God was in the tabernacle because of the shining of the glory of God. The day will come when this world will see the shining of the glory of God again when the sign of the Son of man appears in the heaven. As a light that outshines the brightness of the sun, God's glory will be revealed, and men shall see the sign of the Son of man in the clouds of heaven. What will be their response? When Israel saw the glory of God manifested in their camp, they fell and worshiped; and when the glory of God moved, they followed. But in Revelation 19:19, John says,

> And I saw the beast, and the kings of the earth, and their armies that would include both the kings of the east as well

> as the western confederacy gathered together to make war against him that sat on the horse, and against his army.

When these two military powers are coming to do battle to settle the question as to who will rule the world, suddenly the light of the glory of God will appear in the heavens, and they will recognize this as an invasion—if you please—from outer space. They will recognize that this is God moving in to judge, and those two nations that were ready to battle each other will suddenly join together to fight against the Lord Jesus Christ, the one described in Revelation 19:11-16 as the victorious Commander on the white horse whose name is the King of kings and the Lord of lords. These two groups will never get to use their weapons on each other; they never will fire a shot. The issue as to which one of them will rule the world will never be settled, because the Lord Jesus Christ will come to this earth and, according to Revelation 11:15, "The kingdoms of this world are become the kingdoms of our Lord, and of his Christ; and he shall reign for ever and ever."

This will be the greatest display of military might that the world has ever seen, and if 200 million men can be raised up to control affairs within the Oriental nations, think of how many they would send out when they embark on world conquest. Think of the unnumbered multitudes who will gather together under the authority of the commander of the west. But those nations, even though they join together against the Lord Jesus Christ, will not be able to prevent His return, nor will they be able to thwart His judgment, for a sword shall go out of His mouth and He shall destroy those multiplied millions in a moment of time in order that He might be King of kings and Lord of lords.

In the light of the fact that the final battle of this world's history is to be between the east and the west, it is of great significance that within the last decade the east has broken off completely from the west—China has completely broken with Russia. It is also significant that China will be going through such a time of turmoil that her leaders will have to spend their effort and energy to consolidate their authority within their empire. When God removes restraints and they march to battle they will be going out to meet the one who is the Judge of all men. He will put down all rebellion, destroy all military might, and rule as King of kings and Lord of lords. In the light of these references in the Bible, a whole new dimension is added to the reading of newspapers and magazines as we watch the developments in the east, for God is restraining the kings of the east until He will draw the east and the west into battle. Then Jesus Christ shall put down the mightiest gathering of military men the world has known so that He might demonstrate how great are the authority and the power that belong to His Son.

13

THE FINAL WORLD WAR

IN TEACHING THE DISCIPLES truths concerning His coming back to the earth a second time, our Lord said to them, "Ye shall hear of wars and rumours of wars" (Mt 24:6). The strife that has characterized the nations down through the ages will continue until the Prince of Peace comes to this earth to bring peace. Christ indicated that as we approach the time of His coming, wars will become more frequent, will engulf a greater portion of the earth, will increase in intensity, and during that seven-year period after the translation of the church into glory—a seven-year period called the tribulation period—the world will be divided by wars such as have never occurred previously in human history. Describing this time, Christ said, "For then shall be great tribulation, such as was not since the beginning of the world to this time, no, nor ever shall be" (Mt 24:21).

A great deal of the intensity of this tribulation will come on the earth through the tramp of marching armies. This great final conflict between nations is referred to in the Word of God as the campaign or the Battle of Armageddon. Just the name Armageddon brings to mind the thought of a conflict that beggars description, a conflict unequaled in the annals of human history. As great as have been some of the conflicts that have existed in the past, these will seem as nothing compared to the intensity of the conflagration that will sweep across the earth in this final world war. There will be four separate and distinct movements by the four different world powers or groups of world powers involved in this campaign of Armageddon.

Can any conclusions be drawn concerning the possibility of such a holocaust breaking out very shortly? The focal point of human history is not in Europe, nor in Southeast Asia, nor in Red China, but in Palestine. The prophet Zechariah, who is joined by a multitude of other prophetic witnesses in the Word of God, testifies to the fact that the final world conflagration will not be a conflict or a contest over any of the above-mentioned areas, as strategic as they are in world affairs today. The final conflict will be a contest over the possession of an almost insignificant little piece of real estate known today as Israel or the land of Palestine; and within that small land the armies will be drawn to the city of Jerusalem, which will become the center of the target against which armies from all over the world will be massed.

The prophet uses a very graphic picture in Zechariah 12 as he describes Jerusalem as a millstone under which grain was ground to flour. The prophet said that God would make Jerusalem a burdensome stone (Zec 12:3), that is, a millstone. The city of Jerusalem will become a mill in which the nations will be poured as grist in order that they might be ground under divine judgment as a millstone grinds wheat into flour. God's purpose, according to Zechariah 12:3, is to gather all the people of the earth together against Jerusalem, and all the peoples—all the nations from over the face of the earth—will be gathered together against Jerusalem (v. 9) because God will judge the nations. As observed already, the Gentile nations at the end times will be divided up into four major spheres of influence as far as they affect the program of God—the Arab Block, the first sphere; the king of the north, that is, Russia and her allies, a second power; the third area of influence, the European sphere; and the fourth, the Oriental sphere of influence. In Revelation 16:13 John sees three unclean spirits, demons charged by the prince of the demons with a very important ministry. The three unclean spirits will emerge like frogs out of the mouth of the dragon, the beast, and the false prophet. "They are the spirits of demons working miracles [now notice], which go forth unto the kings of the earth and of the whole world, to gather them to the battle of that great day of God Almighty."

Satan will gather together these four great spheres of world authority in order to attempt to overthrow God and prevent Christ's earthly reign. He will be moving in counsels of state, controlling international politics. He will be moving in summit conferences and in leaders of nations to cause these nations to unleash their fury against the land of Israel. The reason is quite plain. When Jesus Christ comes back to the earth the second time in order to rule, He is going to rule over the nation Israel and the whole world in the land of Palestine. He will set up His throne in David's ancient city, Jerusalem, and He will rule the world from there. Satan, that sly fox, will seek to prevent God's program from coming to its fulfillment by destroying all the Jews and the city from which Jesus Christ will reign so that His reign would be impossible. If His reign is impossible, God is a liar, and what He has promised is not true. Even today there is a satanic influence behind these movements of nations that defies comprehension, and were it not for the Word of God, we would be utterly baffled and completely at a loss to explain events occurring today. The prophet Zechariah says that when Satan begins to stir up nations to bring them together to prevent the earthly reign of the Lord Jesus Christ, He brings these nations together into Israel for the purpose of destroying Jerusalem.

Daniel 11 foretells the first movement against Israel. Satan will unleash these nations and bring their armies against Palestine in the middle of the tribulation period, which will be three and a half years before Christ's second advent to earth to reign. It also will be three and a half years after the church has been translated and caught up into glory. Midway into that seven-year period, this great movement of nations against

Palestine will begin. The tribulation period itself will begin after the rapture when the head of the federated states of Europe will enter into an agreement with the nation Israel, guaranteeing to protect them from any invasion from without so that the west, or the European confederacy, will back Israel against the Arabs and those with whom they are allies, their neighbors to the north, the Russians. Daniel 9 says that period will begin when this one will make a covenant with Israel; and for three and a half years the state of Israel will exist threatened from without. But she will be in a state of cold war, afraid that the nations might come against her, but trusting in her covenant with the European confederacy to protect her.

If such a guarantee should be made with the nation Israel today, the nations of the earth would breathe a great sigh of relief because they know that Palestine is the key to peace or war. The world lives in dread and terror of what will happen if the Arabs decide to go into Israel or if Israel decides to attack an Arab nation. The world is looking for someone who can guarantee peace, and this man who will arise in the European confederacy, who will seem to settle that problem, will be hailed as the world's greatest peace bringer, and he will be honored as a prince of peace. But his covenant will be short-lived. It will last for three and a half years before the covenant will be broken. The first movement in the campaign of Armageddon is described in Daniel 11:40: "And at the time of the end shall the king of the south push at him." The "him" referred to is this western leader, the head of the United States of Europe. Because of his alliance with Israel, any movement against Israel is also a movement against the head of the European confederacy.

For the first three and one half years of this confederacy, the nations will be afraid to move, but finally the king of the south will move against the leader of the western confederacy by moving against Palestine whose national integrity this leader in the western confederacy has guaranteed to preserve.

"The king of the south" refers to Egypt, the land in which Israel had dwelt from the time the patriarchs had gone down there under Jacob and Joseph until they were redeemed and became a nation of some two and a half million people, more than four hundred years later. From then on, Israel could never forget that they were bondslaves in Egypt and that the monarch of Egypt was that king of the land of the south. A study of Ezekiel 38 reveals that the Arab states will be brought together in a federation that could be called the United Arab Republic, and the king of the south, along with those who are federated with him, will move against Palestine and against Jerusalem. This will be the first movement of Armageddon. The Pan-Arab block will move against Israel to destroy it.

As soon as the Pan-Arab block moves into Palestine, they will be joined by the second great invader, Russia. In Ezekiel 38:16, speaking of Gog and the land of Magog, God says,

> And thou shalt come up against my people of Israel, as a cloud to cover the land; it shall be in the latter days, and I will bring thee against my land, that the heathen may know me, when I shall be sanctified in thee, O Gog, before their eyes.

This chapter reveals that there will be a second invasion of Palestine that will take place almost simultaneously with the first invasion by the Arab states, and this is the invasion by a power called "the king of the north." We have already shown why we believe that Gog, the land of Magog, the king of the north, is Russia. Thus, this chapter describes an invasion by the Russian confederacy that here is allied with the Pan-Arab states. The Russian confederacy will desire to capture Palestine so that they can take the spoils of the land (Eze 38:12) and they will entice the Arab states to move against Israel. And when the Arab states move, Russia will immediately move in, and the Arab states coming from the south will be met by the Russian invaders who come from the north and Jerusalem will be totally destroyed.

It will seem as though the prophecies of God have come to nought, that Jerusalem is put under the millstone, and that the nations are grinding Jerusalem as the wheat is ground into flour. But this will only be the first part of the campaign. Who actually is grist for God's mill has not been shown because, according to Ezekiel 38, when these two military powers have joined forces in Jerusalem as allies, after Jerusalem is destroyed they will retreat to the vast plain of Meggido, the plain that stretches across the northern portion of Palestine from Carmel eastward to the Sea of Galilee. That vast plain will become headquarters of the military powers of the Arabs and the Russians who have moved into Palestine. As they encamp there, with Jerusalem a smoldering ruin, they will challenge the world to do anything about it. It is at this time that God will accept the challenge, and He will do with that Arab-Russian alliance what He did with Sodom and Gomorrah, because in Ezekiel 38:22, God said,

> I will rain upon him [Russia], and upon his bands [Allies], and upon the many people that are with him [Pan-Arab block], an overflowing rain, and great hailstones, fire, and brimstone.

God in a moment of time will destroy invader No. 1 and invader No. 2. As a result of this destruction, the world will be in a political vacuum. The power of the Russians and the Arab states will have been broken, which will clear the way for the occupation of the land of Israel by the western confederacy, or the united states of Europe. In Daniel 11, following the invasion by the king of the south and the king of the north (v. 40), a description is given of the third invasion of Palestine. Since Jerusalem is so strategic, and the one who will rule the world must occupy Palestine, the head of the federated states of Europe will leave Europe and move his armies into Palestine to occupy it. In verse 41 this invasion is described. He will enter the glorious land (Palestine), overthrowing many countries in the invasion. The land of Egypt shall not escape; the European head shall have power over the treasures of gold and of silver, and over all the precious things of Egypt.

These two verses suggest that when the European armies invade Palestine, they will do it by crossing the Mediterranean into North Africa, coming across through Egypt, pick up the riches of Egypt on their way across, and come into Palestine from the south. At that time, verse 45 says, "He shall plant the tabernacles of his palace between the seas in the glorious holy mountain." The glorious holy mountain is David's city, David's holy mountain. When the head of the united states of Europe will seek to rule the world from Palestine, he will make Jerusalem his capital. He evidently will have to set up temporary headquarters because Russia and the Arabs will have destroyed Jerusalem. There will be no city there. Notice how specific the prophecy is, for verse 45 says, "He shall plant the tabernacles of his palace between the seas [between the Dead Sea and the Mediterranean] in the glorious holy mountain."

Notice that it does not say he will move into Jerusalem. Jerusalem won't be there. But he will be able to set up his headquarters in that area from which Christ eventually will rule the world. There he will proclaim himself a world dictator. This is described in Revelation 13 and 2 Thessalonians 2 where it says the lawless one will set himself up as God to rule the world. This European military dictator will proclaim himself to be God and king, and he will put himself on a throne from which he will claim to rule the world. And Palestine will then be occupied by this western confederacy. They won't be able to do much in the way of building. They will have to spend their time cleaning up the debris, because Ezekiel 39 says it will take them seven months to bury the corpses that they find in the land and seven years to clean up the debris which will be left behind when God wipes out the northern armies with fire and brimstone. The land will be a desolation, and that which is destined to be a garden under

Messiah's reign will bear all the marks of the carnage of war. In spite of that, this third great invader will move in and occupy Palestine, and rule the world, claiming worldwide authority for the last three and one half years of the tribulation period. It is during this period and through the military movements of this ruler that so much of the earth's surface will be destroyed as described in Revelation.

In Revelation 16 a fourth invader is described. The Word of God has nothing to say about the Orient or these eastern nations and people. Possibly they will be in such a state of turmoil during the tribulation period, that even though one claims to be an absolute world dictator and claims authority over them, they will offer no resistance against this claim on the part of the European confederacy. There seems no other way to explain their silence when the European dictator claims to rule over the whole world. At the end of the tribulation period the sixth angel, one of the instruments of divine judgment during the latter part of the tribulation period, will pour out his vial "upon the great river Euphrates and the water thereof was dried up that the way of the kings of the east might be prepared." The kings of the east are not identified in Scripture other than as coming from beyond the Euphrates River. They will have to be Oriental people who will be kept out of this conflagration taking place in Palestine until God is ready to let them in. And when God is ready, He will send an angel to prepare the way. This Oriental power, called "the king of the east," is coming toward Palestine to contest the European dictator's claim that he is the ruler of the world. These two great powers, the western confederacy and the Oriental nations, will be preparing for a major battle that will take place in Palestine.

At that time a most significant thing will take place. This is referred to in Christ's teaching in Matthew 24:30. When these two great world powers will be marching toward each other, there shall appear the sign of the Son of man in heaven, and then shall all tribes of the earth mourn, and they shall see the Son of man coming in the clouds of heaven and in great glory. When God manifested His presence in Israel in the Old Testament, it was by a shining light. The glory of God was manifested in a pillar of fire or a cloud that glowed, and that light was the sign that God was present in Israel. It is my conviction that as these two military powers are converging against each other, the Lord Jesus Christ will reveal His glory to the earth, and all the nations of the earth will behold His glory, a glory that exceeds the brightness of lightning that cannot be hid. This will be a sign that even these apostate leaders will recognize. They will know that God is moving in to judge them. These two nations that were preparing to fight each other suddenly will join in an agreement to unite their forces to defeat the Lord Jesus Christ when He comes back to this earth. In Revelation 19:11, John saw heaven open and a white horse. He that sat upon him was called faithful and true. On His vesture was the name, the Word of God (v. 13). All the saints and the angels which were in heaven followed Him. "Out of his mouth goeth a sharp sword, that with it he should smite the nations" (v. 15). These are the nations that have agreed together that they will join forces to prevent the second advent of Jesus Christ to this earth and overthrow Him when He comes as King of kings and Lord of lords.

In verse 17, God sends out an invitation to all the vultures and invites them to come to supper, the supper of the great God that they may eat the flesh of kings, of captains, of mighty men, the flesh of horses and them that sit on them, the flesh of all men, free and bond, small and great. "And I saw the beast, and the kings of the earth, and their armies [that would be the western confederacy allied with the Oriental powers], gathered together to make war against him that sat on the horse, and against his army" (v. 19). This will be the fifth invasion of Palestine. The first will be by Egypt and the Arabs; the second by Russia and her European allies; the third by the European confederacy; and the fourth by the kings of the east. The fifth will be the invasion by the Lord of glory from heaven. When He comes, He will come to destroy the nations that are gathered together against Jerusalem. That is when the Lord Jesus Christ will smite the nations with the sword that emerges out of His mouth. Those who followed the beast will be slain with the "sword of him that sat upon the horse, which sword proceeded out of his mouth: and all the fowls were filled with their flesh" (v. 21). Who has become grist in God's mill? The Son of God has dealt one by one with four mighty coalitions of nations, attracting them together to the millstone. He has ground them in His mill. The mill is in Israel, and Jerusalem is the millstone, and the nations that thought they could put God's people and His plan into the mill and grind it to powder will themselves be sucked into that mill and destroyed by the one who has the right to be King of kings and Lord of lords.

These four invasions will all occur within the space of three years and six months. At the end of that time it will be demonstrated to every intelligent creature on earth that Jesus Christ is Lord and besides Him there is no other, that He is King of kings and Lord of lords.

There is a question that has been asked innumerable times: Where does the United States fit into this prophecy? Some students of prophecy have concluded that because the United States is not specifically mentioned in this final conflagration of nations she will have passed out of existence. Some have gone so far as to say that God will deliver the United States into the hand of the Communists to chasten us for our apostasy and ungodliness. I don't deny that we deserve it and that God would be justified in using such a nation to destroy us because of our wickedness and independence of God. But I offer this alternative suggestion: In chapters 2 and 7 of Daniel, when the prophet describes the fourth empire, he saw that empire as an empire that would be divided into ten toes or horns. The power that was in Rome was divided among many emerging nations. When the final Gentile world ruler rules in Europe, he will unite under his authority nations that emerged out of the old Roman Empire. Now what is our origin? Politically, socially, economically and linguistically, we have come from nations that originally belonged to the old Roman Empire. Our customs and laws have all come from that European background, from nations that have emerged out of the Roman Empire. Daniel speaks of those nations as the ten horns or the ten toes that will be brought together under the power and the authority of the beast. Even though we are not one of the ten by virtue of the fact that we did not emerge directly out of the Old Roman Empire, we may be one of the ten by virtue of our heritage. The United States may well cast her lot with Europe and come into this confederation of nations and be a part of that western confederacy that will be drawn into this conflict and will be judged by the Lord at His second advent.

How near is all of this? The very recital of these four invasions and invaders will bring the conviction to any individual that even though we do not know how long it may be, it need not be long. It could take place at anytime. We read daily of the conflicts between Israel and some of the Arab nations. Russia is ready to go; they have laid the groundwork. They have made their overtures to the Arab states and, almost without exception, the Arabs are looking to the north, not the west, for help. Europe is coming closer and closer together through the Common Market. These things are things which could take place almost overnight. We are standing on the brink of such movements. The stage is so completely and perfectly set that they could take place at any moment. Only one thing holds it up, and that is that you and I are here. God is restraining and holding it back. God couldn't pour out judgments upon Sodom and Gomorrah until the righteous ones were taken out, but just as soon as those righteous ones left, the judgment came. God could not release the judgments in Noah's day until those believers were safely in the ark. These judgments will not be released upon the earth as long as believers are here. This is not to say there could not be other world wars, if God delayed a little longer. Since the stage is so set, God at any moment could lift that curtain, take us to Himself, and let this program come to its prophesied conclusion. "Lift up your heads for your redemption draweth nigh" (Lk 21:28).

14

GOD'S PLAN FOR WORLD EVANGELIZATION DURING THE TRIBULATION

AT THE RAPTURE of the church, God, in a moment, in the twinkling of an eye, will snatch every believer in the Lord Jesus Christ out of this earth and bring them into glory. When that translation has been completed there will not be a single individual on the earth who acknowledges Jesus Christ as his personal Saviour, not one who personally knows the salvation that God has provided through Christ, not a person who has God's answer to the problem of sin, who knows experientially the way to eternal life. Those left on earth will be those who were ignorant of God's salvation and consequently in unbelief, or those who rejected the gospel and were under judgment. The tribulation period—a period of apostasy, unbelief, and rejection of Jesus Christ as personal Saviour—will begin. The world will truly be in its darkest hour.

Yet, according to Revelation 7, seven years later there will be a multitude which no man can number of all nations and kindreds and people and tongues who will stand before the throne and before the Lamb robed with white robes, with palms in their hands crying, saying, "Salvation to our God which sitteth upon the throne, and unto the Lamb" (v. 10). When John beheld that great multitude he could not identify them, and the question is asked in verse 13, "What are these which are arrayed in white robes? And whence came they?" John had to confess his ignorance. He does so by addressing the elder, saying, "Thou knowest." Then the explanation is given to John:

> These are they which came out of great tribulation, and have washed their robes, and made them white in the blood of the Lamb (v. 14).

Think of it. Seven years before, not a single individual on earth knew Jesus Christ as personal Saviour or knew the plan of salvation, but at the end of that seven-year period there is an innumerable multitude from every nation on the face of the earth who have washed their robes and made them white in the blood of the Lamb. Something supernatural has been taking place, for this cannot be explained naturally. God has a program to bring multitudes to Himself, and this program will be accomplished within a seven-year period.

Just before John was shown this scene in heaven of these innumerable multitudes who had washed their robes and made them white in the blood of the Lamb, he was given a picture of the sealing of the servants of God (vv. 3-8). John saw 12,000 from each of the twelve tribes of Israel being set apart by God. They were sealed in their foreheads. In Scripture, a seal is a mark of identification; and God supernaturally and sovereignly put His identifying mark upon these 144,000 physical descendants of Abraham. The fact that they received God's identifying seal in their foreheads means that they were being set apart to Him. This is a mark of ownership. It is also a mark that guarantees preservation, and John was told that nothing could happen to these 144,000 because God was preserving them for that for which they were called (v. 3).

We believe these 144,000 are exactly what the Scripture says—144,000 physical descendants of Abraham, 12,000 from each of the twelve tribes. The objector says that no physical descendant of Abraham knows his tribal lineage. How can we have 144,000 Israelites so set apart by God when nobody knows their tribal inheritance? While an individual may not know his tribal inheritance, God certainly does. Up until the time of the destruction of the temple in A.D. 70, the rolls were carefully kept according to the laws of Levitical inheritance so that every physical descendant of Abraham had a tribal inheritance and tribal lineage, and each could consult the scrolls if there were any doubt about his inheritance. Since that time those records have been kept in the mind of almighty God so that God can fulfill His purpose in His own time.

A further objection is frequently raised that this is impossible because ten tribes have been lost. That is a figment of the imagination. There is no such thing as ten lost tribes. Satan is trying to blind the minds of men as to the purpose and program of God. You remember that the ten tribes went into captivity to Assyria in 722 B.C., and that the two southern tribes went into captivity in Babylon in 586 B.C. But when the seventy years of the Babylonian captivity were over, as recorded in the books of Ezra and Nehemiah, representatives from all twelve tribes came back. Not just representatives from the two southern tribes that went into Babylon, but representatives from the twelve tribes came back into the land, and were reestablished in the land, and had their inheritance in the land. Ezra 2:70 says "all Israel" returned. When someone says God can't possibly fulfill this prophecy because ten tribes have been lost and nobody knows where they are, not even God, then that person is ignorant of Scripture, denying the purpose that God has for His people Israel.

When God chose Israel as His own people He chose them, according to Exodus 19:16, to be "a kingdom of priests." He chose them to be His representatives, and Israel in the Old Testament was the light of the world. Israel was to carry the light of the knowledge of God to the Gentile nations around them. Israel did not fulfill that function for which they were set apart by God. Therefore, when the New Testament opens, as it is recorded by the apostle John, Christ came as the true light that lightens every man that comes into the world. Christ came to bring the knowledge of God to nations that were in darkness. He came to perform that function that God had originally entrusted to the nation Israel. That is why He is called the true light as opposed to Israel, who was a false light. God who chose the nation to perform a special function will one day perform that function through that very people, and it is to that end that John sees God sealing 144,000 representatives of the twelve tribes so that they in that day can fulfill that purpose for which God originally chose them, that they should be light to the world.

In 1 Corinthians 15:8 is a clue concerning the way God will work after the church's rapture. After the apostle has listed those to whom the resurrected Christ appeared, so as to authenticate His resurrection, he says, "And last of all he was seen of me also, as of one born out of due time." This phrase "born out of due time" means a premature birth. That is exactly what the apostle Paul is saying—"I was one that was born prematurely." What did he mean? Comparing Revelation 7 with Paul's statement in 1 Corinthians 15 we conclude that after the rapture of the church, God will perform the same miracle He performed in Saul of Tarsus on the Damascus Road 144,000 times over. The experience that Paul had on the road to Damascus is what these 144,000 will experience in that day when God sovereignly reveals Himself to these descendants of Abraham and brings them to Himself. Notice a parallelism. Saul of Tarsus had his religion. He was perfectly satisfied with it. He was zealous in it. He had risen to prominence in his generation because he was so zealous and so knowledgeable, and yet he did not know Christ. He had the ability, the talent, the personality, the education, and the experience to be a witness for Christ. He had everything but Christ. And when Christ revealed Himself to Saul of Tarsus, it was no time at all before Paul was preaching. God sovereignly brought him to Himself and equipped him and used him as an instrument to bring the gospel not to Israel but to the Gentiles.

And what Christ did for Saul of Tarsus He will do 144,000 times over to call and equip and empower these witnesses so that they can bring the gospel to every kindred and tongue and tribe and nation. It will take a sovereign work such as this because after the rapture of the church, believers will be gone. There will be no missionaries, no evangelists, no preachers, no witnessing church here. There will be an apostate, Christ-rejecting church; but they will not suddenly become evangelists for Jesus Christ. God has no use for them at all. How then are men going to hear? God will convert and equip these physical descendants of Abraham so that they can go to every nation and kindred and people and tongue and declare the gospel to them.

The gospel that they will preach is described in Revelation 7:14 in the explanation of who this multitude is: "They . . . have washed their robes, and made them white in the blood of the Lamb." And the gospel that will be preached in that day is the gospel of salvation by faith through grace based on the blood of Christ. They will not preach a different gospel than that which redeems today. There is not another gospel that differs from the good news that Christ died for our sins. God has only one plan of salvation, and that centers in the death of His Son, and God will reveal the plan of salvation through the Word of God to these 144,000 whom He seals. God will empower them by the Holy Spirit and, in that energy of the Holy Spirit, equipped with the knowledge of the gospel of salvation by grace through faith, they will go to every kindred and tongue and tribe and nation and declare the gospel that will convert a multitude and bring them to Jesus Christ.

Something of the economy of God's operation can be seen here. Any missionary going to a foreign field will spend his first term on the field learning the language. Remember that in the tribulation period God only has seven years, and if five of it had to be spent learning the language, that would not allow much time to get the job done. Here is the economy of God's operation. In every nation, in every language, there are physical descendants of Abraham who, if they knew Jesus

Christ, would already be prepared to preach and to teach. They know the language, the culture, the customs, the people. They are already established. God will reach down in every kindred and tongue and tribe and nation and take some of these that have been there and know the people, the culture, the language, and they will be able, immediately after this revelation and empowerment by the Spirit, to be in the ministry of telling people that they can wash their robes and make them white in the blood of the Lamb.

For the first three and one half years of the tribulation these who have been sovereignly converted and sent to minister the gospel all over the world will have little response. At the beginning of the tribulation, the head of the federated states of Europe will be elevated to power and he will offer peace to the world, and will present himself as the prince of peace. Men will follow him, taking the attitude that since this political leader guarantees them peace and gives them prosperity, they don't need God at all. These 144,000 witnesses will preach the gospel of salvation by grace through faith and will be laughed at and ridiculed.

But God isn't finished yet. In Revelation 11:3-7 is a description of those whom God calls "my two witnesses." These are witnesses raised up by God to support and to authenticate the ministry of the 144,000 evangelists or missionaries proclaiming the gospel. From Revelation 11:1-2 it is quite obvious that these two witnesses minister in Jerusalem, that is, the literal city of Jerusalem which, according to Daniel 11, is made the world dictator's headquarters. These two witnesses minister for 1,260 days or three and one half years, which would be the last half of the tribulation period.

They appear, "clothed in sackcloth" (v. 3). John the Baptist appeared in the desert with a camel's hair garment; that was sackcloth. The Old Testament prophets clothed themselves with sackcloth. It was a sign of mourning and repentance, and when these two prophets appear clothed in sackcloth, by their very garb they will be calling people to repentance, to confession of sins. They will be preaching the same thing John preached when he said, "Repent ye: for the kingdom of heaven is at hand" (Mt 3:2). And these two witnesses are called "the two olive trees, and the two candlesticks standing before the God of the earth" (v. 4).

In the prophet Zechariah's day, the nation was facing a very troublous time. They had started to rebuild the temple after the Babylonian captivity, and adversaries were opposing the work. God brought comfort by telling Zechariah that the work would be accomplished "not by might, nor by power, but by my spirit" (4:6). God had sent two Spirit-empowered men, Joshua and Zerubbabel, to lead the nation in this work. Joshua was the high priest, and Zerubbabel was the governmental ruler. Through their Spirit-prompted ministry, they were to assist Israel in the rebuilding of the temple.

In Revelation 11 God says He will send two men, empowered by the Spirit, and they will prepare Israel for the one who will rebuild the temple—the Lord Jesus Christ. These two witnesses will be able to perform miracles to prove their divine authority. First, there will be miracles to preserve themselves. "If any man will hurt them, fire proceedeth out of their mouth, and devoureth their enemies: and if any man will hurt them, he must in this manner be killed" (v. 5). They will destroy by fire those who oppose their ministry. "These have power to shut heaven, that it rain not in the days of their prophecy." (v. 6). Remember that when Elijah appeared before Ahab, the sign that he was God's prophet was that he told Ahab that it would not rain for three and one half years. Thus, these men will be able to perform miracles as Elijah performed them. Further, "they have power over waters to turn them to blood, and to smite the earth with all plagues, as often as they will." That is reminiscent of Moses' miracles which he performed before Pharaoh to prove it was God who gave the order to let His people go. Many believe that these two witnesses are Moses and Elijah who will be reincarnated. Others say the two are Enoch and Moses, two

Old Testament saints who were translated into glory without dying. We believe these men are not resurrected individuals, but two men whom God will raise up and empower in this manner so that they can perform miracles like those of Elijah and Moses in order to authenticate their testimony.

Other events will break down men's resistance to the preaching of the 144,000. In the middle of the tribulation period, the king of the south, the Pan-Arab states, will move against Jerusalem, and the king of the north will move against Palestine. As these two world powers converge on Jerusalem, they will destroy the city and then retreat to the mountains of Israel or to the plains of Esdralon and, according to Ezekiel 38—39, God will rain fire and brimstone upon the kings of the north and the south, and utterly destroy these world powers. We believe that just prior to the destruction of these kings, the two witnesses will stand up in Jerusalem; and when these armies approach they will announce that God will destroy these nations. The people will scoff at them even as they have laughed at the message of salvation they have been preaching, but God shall sovereignly destroy the Russian-Arab confederacy of nations, and Ezekiel says that all the nations will know that they were destroyed by the hand of God. These two witnesses will have foretold what God was going to do and, in fact, they may be the ones who call down the fire of God upon these armies and destroy them, and this evidence of divine authority will be used by God to awaken many to the preaching of the 144,000. For three and one half years they have been preaching with little response. But when these two witnesses stand up and call down fire on the Russian army so that God wipes them out, people will have to listen to the message of the witnesses and the 144,000 and, as a result, multitudes will turn to the Lord.

God will work yet again to bring men to their knees. In the last half of the tribulation period seven angels will sound seven trumpets, and each trumpet is a calamitous judgment. We believe that before any angel will sound his trumpet, these witnesses will call for judgment from heaven. In so doing these two witnesses will support the ministry of the 144,000 as they tell men that God is a God who will judge sin, and the only way to escape that judgment is to wash their robes and make them white in the blood of the Lamb. That message will be so hated by the political-religious ruler, the beast, that he will try to exterminate them; but God won't let them be touched until His time comes.

> And when they shall have finished their testimony, the beast that ascendeth out of the bottomless pit shall make war against them, and shall overcome them, and kill them. And their bodies shall lie in the street of the great city, which spiritually is called Sodom and Egypt, where also our Lord was crucified [Jerusalem]. And they of the people and kindreds and tongues and nations shall see their dead bodies three days and an half (Rev 11:7-9).

People will be rapturously happy that the beast has triumphed over these who were making their life so miserable, and they will have an exchange of gifts to celebrate. While they are watching those corpses in the street, something happens:

> And after three days and an half the spirit of life from God entered into them, and they stood upon their feet; and great fear fell upon them which saw them (v. 11).

This is the sign of Jonah. The same thing that authenticated the Lord Jesus Christ will authenticate these witnesses. Even as Christ's resurrection proved He was the Son of God, these ambassadors will be proved by their resurrection. All of the kindreds, nations, tongues and peoples that saw their unburied corpses will witness their resurrection and, as a result, great fear will fall on them, and multitudes who have been rejecting the gospel up to that point will then turn to Christ. That is God's method of bringing those unnumbered multitudes to Himself. When Christ comes to earth and His feet touch the Mount of Olives, there will be these innumerable multitudes who have come out of the great tribulation. They will have found salvation because God sent the 144,000 witnesses whose ministry was undergirded by the divine authority of the two witnesses and through these combined witnesses, these innumerable multitudes were saved within such a short span of time. It is God's grace that goes to such ends to bring salvation to a world that had already rejected the gospel and, as a consequence, were left behind at the rapture.

Some may say that if God has a program and will accomplish it so marvelously, why should we bother today? Why not leave it up to God? Why should we send more missionaries? Why should we have evangelistic services? Why should we do anything personally about reaching men for Christ? The answer is simple. We do it simply because He told us to. "Ye shall be witnesses unto me" (Ac 1:8). "Go ye into all the world" (Mk 16:15). That is His commission. God has put us as lights in the midst of this crooked and perverse generation. We are not responsible for any past generation nor do we have any responsibility to a future generation. We have a responsibility to this generation of which we are a part. And God has commanded us who know Jesus Christ as personal Saviour to bear witness to men so that they might be saved today. What God will do in the future as He has revealed it in the prophetic program gives no excuse to any child of God to be indifferent to his responsibility to bring the gospel to lost men now.

15

WHEN CHRIST'S FEET TOUCH THE MOUNT OF OLIVES

WITH GOD there is no such thing as unfinished business. That which God has promised and purposed, He most certainly will do. When God makes a promise, that promise is as certain as the character of God Himself. That which was left unfinished of God's prophesied program at the time of Christ's death will be accomplished when He returns to this earth. It was a perplexed group of men whom Christ brought to the crest of the Mount of Olives forty days after His crucifixion:

> And while they looked steadfastly toward heaven as he went up, behold, two men stood by them in white apparel; which also said, Ye men of Galilee, why stand ye gazing up into heaven? This same Jesus, which is taken up from you into heaven, shall so come in like manner as ye have seen him go into heaven (Ac 1:10).

The eyes of these men were fixed upon the clouds as though they were hoping that somehow there would come a rift in the clouds that had separated the Lord Jesus from them, and they could catch a glimpse of Him as He was disappearing into glory. But the angels announced that though men could not see Jesus Christ ascend into glory they would see Him return. The promise was very clear: "This same Jesus, which is taken up from you into heaven, shall so come in like manner as ye have seen him go into heaven."

In the upper-room discourse in John 13—17, Christ had told the disciples that He was going away from them and that He would return again. He was speaking of His physical death on the cross of Calvary, and He told those men that He would leave them in death. But He also told them that He would return to them by resurrection. Then He gave another promise: "Again, I will go away, and I will come again." This time the going away was the ascension, and the coming again was the second advent or His return to the earth. So there was a preparation for the incident recorded in Acts 1. Christ took them to the Mount of Olives, and suddenly a cloud received Him out of their sight. He who had been with them, speaking with them, commissioning them to go and be His witnesses, was not there anymore. He had gone into glory. In order to assuage their grief, God dispatched angels with a message of comfort and hope: "This same Jesus . . . shall so come."

Jesus went away by physical death, and He came back again by resurrection. Ten saw Him in the upper room, and they knew that it was the same Jesus; but Thomas, who was absent, could not conceive of the fact that one who had been taken away could return. So Jesus appeared to Thomas and, to prove to him that He was the same man, He showed him His hands and side. Then Thomas knew that this same Jesus—who had gone to the cross, whose body had been placed in the tomb—had come back again. Now as Christ is received up into glory and a cloud veils Him from their natural eyes, the angel says, "This same Jesus shall come again." Not one similar to Him, but this same one will come again, and He will come in like manner "as ye have seen him go into heaven." Jesus Christ was personally received up into glory, and He shall personally come to this earth the second time.

The skeptic or doubter, who does not believe that Jesus Christ is the eternal Son of God and who has no confidence in the promise of God's Word, says that the Holy Spirit's coming at Pentecost was Christ's second coming. Or he thinks that when one believes in Jesus (whatever that means to them—it means something entirely different than Christ meant when

He told Nicodemus he had to believe on Him), Jesus comes into his heart a second time. Or they say that if you experience some tragedy or if some calamity befalls you, Jesus is near you to comfort and cheer. That is the second coming.

Those explanations do not satisfy the requirements of this passage, because the angel said, "This same Jesus shall come as ye have seen him go." As He left personally, He personally is coming back the second time. Jesus Christ was received up into heaven bodily. That resurrected, glorified body that the disciples had seen and had touched, whose voice they had heard, was received up into glory. It was bodily ascension, and it is the comfort of every child of God to know that there is a glorified man in heaven now. He went bodily, and He is coming back bodily; and His glorified body will stand again on the Mount of Olives and walk through the land over which He walked before. The very same mount that witnessed His departure will witness His return. The Mount of Olives was the mount where the disciples so often had retired with our Lord, where He had sat with them and talked with them, where they had overheard Him praying on their behalf. It was a scene very dear to their hearts. It was to that mount that our Lord took the disciples so that they might witness this ascension, and it is to this very spot that the Lord Jesus Christ is coming again.

This is made clear in Zechariah 14, where several significant events are described which will take place when the feet of the Lord Jesus touch the Mount of Olives again. In Zechariah 14:1-3, the prophet has described the warfare that will take place in Palestine and particularly in Jerusalem in the latter part of the tribulation period. During that time there will be four great invasions by four military powers of the land of Palestine. This military movement will begin, according to Daniel 11, when the king of the south, or the Pan-Arab block, invades the Holy Land. They will be joined almost immediately by the king of the north (Eze 38, Dan 12), whom we believe to be Russia and Russia's allies. These two military powers will have consented to invade Palestine to plunder the riches of that land.

After that twofold invasion those two coalitions will be destroyed by God in the same way that God destroyed Sodom and Gomorrah. The land of Palestine then will be occupied by the third invader under the leadership of the beast or the head of the federated states of Europe (Dan 11). Palestine will become a military camp and be occupied by the armies of the west, who will continue in authority over Palestine until their right to rule is challenged by the king of the east (Rev 16), leading an army made up of Oriental peoples. Coming from beyond the Euphrates River, they will move toward Palestine to occupy and control it. This great military movement, referred to in Scripture as the campaign of Armageddon, is summarized in Zechariah 14:1-3. In verse 2 the prophet says, "I will gather all nations against Jerusalem to battle." As these nations move into that land, God will destroy them and remove them from the earth. This judgment is described in Revelation 19:11-16 where Christ at His second advent is pictured as a conquering general invading on a white horse. When He invades this earth's sphere as the rider on the white horse, "out of his mouth goeth a sharp sword, that with it he should smite the nations: and he shall rule them with a rod of iron" (v. 15) and His name is "KING OF KINGS, AND LORD OF LORDS" (v. 16). In Zechariah 14:6-7, in describing the day of His coming, the prophet mentions a significant fact:

> And it shall come to pass in that day, that the light shall not be clear, nor dark: but it shall be one day which shall be known to the LORD, not day, nor night: but it shall come to pass, that at evening time it shall be light.

The prophet describes some great change that takes place in the heavens so that the earth is bathed in light throughout a twenty-four-hour period. There is an extended twilight. The explanation for this is:

> Immediately after the tribulation of those days shall the sun be darkened, and the moon shall not give her light, and the stars shall fall from heaven, and the powers of the heavens shall be shaken (Mt 24:29-30).

Lucifer, at the time of his original rebellion against God, wanted to rule over God's universe. He wanted to control the earth and the stars and all the heavenly bodies and bring them under his authority. But he was not the creator, and he could not change the course of the stars nor change the orbit of any of the heavenly bodies. But God is the Creator and He can control that which He created. In connection with the second advent of Christ, there will be a great convulsion in the heavens in which the one who holds all things together by the word of His power (Heb 1) will change the natural orbit in which the heavenly bodies have been moving since the time of their creation by the Word of God. God will touch the sun so that it shall be darkened and the moon shall not give her light, and the stars shall fall from heaven so that there will be no starlight. The earth will have every source of natural light removed at the time Christ comes. That would suggest that the earth would be plunged into total darkness, for if the sun ceases its shining and there is no moon and there are no stars, there would be nothing but darkness that would envelop the earth.

> And then shall appear the sign of the Son of man in heaven: and then shall all the tribes of the earth mourn, and they shall see the Son of man coming in the clouds of heaven with power and great glory (Mt 24:30).

Matthew records Christ's word that there will be a sign in the heavens that will serve notice to those on the earth that God is present on the earth again. The Lord does not explain His word, nor does He identify the sign of the Son of man in heaven, but it is possible to draw certain conclusions as to what this sign of the Son of man that appears in the heavens actually is. In Exodus 40, after Moses had erected the tabernacle and set the furniture in place and had completed what God had ordained, the glory of the Lord filled the tabernacle. The glory of the Lord manifests itself by the shining of light. It is referred to as the Shekinah, or the glory of the Lord. The tabernacle became a vehicle which manifested God's presence among them as it shone with the glory of God. When Solomon erected the temple (1 Ki 8) and the ark had been put in place, the glory of the Lord filled the temple. It was the same glory that revealed God's presence in the tabernacle. In the wilderness, when God wanted the children of Israel to strike camp and move, He went before them; and His presence was revealed through the pillar of cloud or the pillar of fire.

With this observation in mind, a conclusion can be drawn concerning the sign of the Son of man in heaven. When the sun has withdrawn its light, the moon has ceased its shining, the stars shine no more on the earth, and the earth is in that darkness, suddenly the Light of the world will penetrate that darkness, the Son of God will come as the Prince of Glory to manifest His glory on the earth. That darkness will be dissipated and dispelled in the same way in which the darkness of the holy of holies in the tabernacle was dispelled by the presence of the glory of God in it. The Son of God will appear in the heavens, manifesting to the earth the glory of God, and the darkness will be dispelled and the earth will be bathed in light, not the light of a created sun or moon, but the light of the uncreated eternal Son of God. Then it can be said that that spoken by Isaiah the prophet is fulfilled, Immanuel has come. God is with us. And the nations that were gathered together to fight against each other will see that light from the glory of God and will join together to seek to prevent Christ's return. That is what Zechariah is prophesying when he says that at the time of the Lord's return, "It shall come to pass . . . that the light shall not be clear, nor dark . . . it shall be one day . . . known to the LORD, not day, nor night" (14:6-7). The earth will not be illuminated by the sun by day nor the moon by night, but continuously through the cycle of time, Christ will give light to the earth, and the one who at His first coming said, "I am the light of the world" (Jn 8:12) will cause the light of His glory to bathe this earth, and men shall walk in His light.

In Revelation 21:23 the apostle John says that the heavenly city, the new Jerusalem, needs neither sun nor moon because the Lamb is the light of it, and this earth will not need sun nor moon because Christ will cause the light of the glory of God to shine upon the earth, and the nations who are received into His earthly millennial kingdom will walk in the light of His countenance. That is one great result of the coming of Christ: He will dispel darkness and bring light to the earth.

In Zechariah 14:4 another significant event is mentioned: "His feet shall stand in that day upon the mount of Olives." When God brought Joshua and the children of Israel into the promised land, He told him, "All the land is before you, and every place that the sole of your foot shall tread upon, I will give it to you." They had to appropriate the land before it became their possession, and the placing of the feet was the act of appropriation. This earth belongs to God. It is His by creation, and it is His by redemption because Jesus Christ came not only to redeem man from sin, but to redeem this earth, which has been cursed by man's sin, from sin. But the earth will not become God's possession until the Son of God plants His feet on it and possesses it in God's name. When Columbus touched these shores for the first time, he planted his feet and the flag on the land and claimed it in the name of the queen who had sent him; and when Jesus Christ comes to the earth the second time it will be to plant His feet on the Mount of Olives. That will be an act of appropriation in which Christ, who came to redeem the world from sin, will reclaim the world and make it God's possession by that reclamation. But then when His feet touch the Mount of Olives, there will be a catastrophe to the mount itself.

> And the mount of Olives shall cleave in the midst thereof toward the east and toward the west, and there shall be a very great valley; and half of the mountain shall remove toward the north, and half of it toward the south (Zec 14:4).

The Mount of Olives, located just adjacent to Jerusalem, is the highest point in that part of Judea. That is why the pilgrim always spoke of going *up* to Jerusalem. The city was located on the top of the hill, and any invader had to come across deep valleys to attack it. It is impossible to water that area with irrigation from rivers or streams because the mountains are so steep and the water would drain away. This land could not be productive; it is called "the wilderness of Judea." It was an inhospitable, barren, desolate land even though the soil was rich. Yet God, tells of a transformation in the land's topography that will make it possible to fulfill the prophecy of Isaiah 35: The wilderness shall blossom as the rose; the desert shall become a watered garden. How can God turn that desert into a watered garden if the mountains are unchanged? But when Christ's feet touch the Mount of Olives there will be a division of the mountain and a leveling of the land so that Jerusalem, following Christ's return, will be located in the center of a vast plain, a well-watered garden which will become the center of Christ's earthly reign.

A news magazine reported some time ago that a large hotel chain has sent a crew of engineers and geologists to Jerusalem to explore the possibility of building a hotel on the top of the Mount of Olives. After their exploration they reported that the site was a poor place to build because the Mount of Olives is the center of a geological fault and an earthquake in that area might divide the mount and a hotel would certainly be destroyed. So they decided against building there and found another piece of property in another area. Subsequently another hotel was erected on the Mount of Olives which provides a breathtaking view of the old city of Jerusalem. Several years ago we went into that hotel. As we were registering I asked the clerk, "Do you have earthquake insurance on this hotel?" He, of course, did not have the faintest idea why I was asking such a question and wanted to know if I wanted to purchase insurance.

I knew that was to be the place where Christ's feet would one day touch and that when they do, He will demonstrate His authority over this earth by causing the mountains to be moved in order that He might set up His kingdom in the midst of just such land as Isaiah describes where the wilderness blossoms as the rose. The Lord Jesus Christ is the Creator, but men have not been willing to acknowledge that He is Creator. They have denied His essential right to rule by attributing creation to evolution, and this doctrine has deluded men into believing that God had nothing to do with creation. They have robbed Christ of His right to rule.

When Christ returns, He will not be bent on the destruction of Palestine. He will be demonstrating that He created and that He can reform this sin-cursed earth into that which can serve His purpose and reflect His glory. When Christ rules on the earth there will be no desert, no wilderness, no unproductive lands. This earth shall demonstrate the touch of Christ's authority as He transforms this earth to what it was before being cursed by Adam's sin. So, when Christ comes to earth the second time, He shall not only possess it, but He also will refashion it so it will be a suitable sphere in which He will rule.

The third thing mentioned in this passage is that when the Lord's feet touch the Mount of Olives,

> living waters shall go out from Jerusalem; half of them toward the former sea, and half of them toward the hinder sea: in summer and winter shall it be (Zec 14:8).

A traveler passing through Palestine today notices that for the great part of the year there are only dry stream beds. Only for a few weeks does water flow. Then it runs off, leaving the land dry. There is no permanent source of water. But in that day God will provide an abundant source of water so that the land shall become a garden. During Christ's millennial reign, God will have His own method of meeting the problem of famine, poverty and hunger by turning the whole earth into productive land. There will be bounty for all, and Christ will supply streams in the desert. While Christ supplies "streams in the desert" for the believer today in a spiritual sense, the prophet was referring to what the Son of God will do physically when He comes to earth. Looking down the corridors of time to the provision that the Messiah will make for the land when He comes, Ezekiel writes of this same provision:

> Afterward he brought me again unto the door of the house; and, behold, waters issued out from under the threshold of the house eastward: for the forefront of the house stood toward the east, and the waters came down from under from the right side of the house, at the south side of the altar. Then brought he me out of the way of the gate northward, and led me about the way without unto the utter gate by the way that looketh eastward; and, behold, there ran out waters on the right side. And when the man that had the line in his hand went forth eastward, he measured a thousand cubits, and he brought me through the waters; the waters were to the ankles. Again he measured a thousand, and brought me through the waters; the waters were to the knees. Again he measured a thousand, and brought me through; the waters were to the loins. Afterward he measured a thousand; and it was a river that I could not pass over: for the waters were risen, waters to swim in, a river that could not be passed over (47:1-5).

And along the river were trees growing that provided for the health of the nation as described in Revelation 22:1-2. Ezekiel was anticipating the provision which Christ will make for the bounty and the plenty that will come during His reign. The Lord promised that the one who believes on Him, out of his innermost being would flow rivers of water (Jn 7:38). So when Christ returns, the earth will be a watered paradise because He who has provided spiritual waters to slake our thirst will provide the physical water for the earth's productivity.

Israel today has gone to great lengths to bring water from the headwaters of the Sea of Galilee through Israel into the Negev, the desert, to turn it into a productive land. While this provides for them today, when the Lord Jesus Christ comes and His feet touch the Mount of Olives, He will transform the whole land so that rivers will flow and the entire land will be watered. Zechariah shows that what Christ has done for us spiritually, He will do for this earth physically. He has redeemed us; He will come to redeem the earth. He has recreated us; He will come to recreate the earth. He has provided us the water of life; He will come to provide living waters for the earth. He has pledged that He will supply our every need; He will provide for the needs of those who are trusting Him when He comes to this earth the second time.

"The earth is the LORD's" the psalmist said, "and the fulness thereof; the world, and they that dwell therein" (Ps 24:1). This earth has never seen what God can do with it because it has been held in the grips of an usurper. But the Lord is coming personally, visibly and physically in His glorified body to possess it and redeem it from Satan's grasp, to transform and remake it into an instrument that can be used for His glory. And the earth shall be full of the glory and the knowledge of the Lord as the waters cover the sea. When He manifests the glory of God to this earth, we will be with Him, sharing His reign and being used as instruments to bring glory to Him. We shall see Him display His power.

16

SEPARATING THE SHEEP FROM THE GOATS

WHEN ISRAEL'S LEADERS questioned Christ's authority, He affirmed that God had given Him authority to execute judgment because He is the Son of man (Jn 5:22). Christ could claim no greater authority than the authority to judge man, for the one who sits in judgment is superior to those being judged. Since Christ will be judge of all men, obviously He is superior to all. In anticipating the glory that shall be revealed at His second advent, Christians are prone to forget that the one coming as King of kings and Lord of lords is also coming as Judge. Before He can establish His kingdom and ascend the throne and rule, He must remove every obstacle to His reign. John 5 has affirmed the fact that Christ has the right to judge, a right that was conferred upon Him by the Father. Matthew 25 describes the judgment which Christ will execute when He comes to this earth the second time. The fact that Christ is the Judge of all men is so indelibly written on the hearts of men that they recoil at the mention of His coming. While a child of God anticipates Christ's coming and looks forward to it as a blessed hope, the mention of His coming to an unbeliever might cause him to draw back and cringe in fear because he instinctively knows that Jesus Christ is a judge, and he is not prepared to face Him in judgment.

The fact that Christ is a judge scarcely needs to be proved, because it is so generally recognized. But Matthew describes two judgments that take place at Christ's second advent. The first judgment is described in 25:1-30. It is a judgment on living Israelites, those physical descendants of Abraham who had received the promises and covenants of God, in which He asserted that He would send the Messiah who would provide redemption and then would gather the redeemed together, set up a kingdom for them, and rule over them as their King. The Old Testament prophets made it clear that no unsaved person could enter the kingdom which the Lord Jesus Christ will establish on this earth when He comes the second time. That is why Christ said to Nicodemus, "Ye must be born again." Apart from a new birth, Christ said to him, one cannot see the kingdom of God. Christ was only summarizing what the Old Testament prophets had taught, that when Messiah comes He must cause all men to pass under His judgment in order that He might remove the rebel and exclude the unbeliever, and that He might receive into His kingdom those who have trusted Him for salvation.

In the parable of the wise and foolish virgins, the Lord is teaching that the nation Israel, the physical descendants of Abraham, must be subjected to a judgment. Those who have light and life will be received into His kingdom. Those without light and life will be excluded. The ten virgins were divided into two groups. Five were wise, and five were foolish. Notice that all ten had one thing in common: all had lamps. But there the similarity ceases. The possession of lamps suggests that all had an opportunity, a chance to hear, a message delivered to them that salvation had been provided; but not all had availed themselves of the offered salvation. While all had lamps, they were divided on the basis of what they had in their lamps. Five were foolish because their lamps were empty. They had no oil, the source of light. Light was the sign of life, and Christ says in this parable that there would be those in Israel who had an opportunity to know the truth of God's Word and to receive the salvation provided through Christ, but they had not availed themselves of that opportunity and were without light and life. They therefore were excluded. On the other hand, there were those who had the opportunity and they responded to it. They received the offered salvation. They are pictured as having oil in their lamps. They had light, and light was the sign of life; thus the Lord in this first parable tells that when He comes at the second advent He will judge the nation Israel to separate believers from unbelievers, to exclude the unbelievers from the kingdom He will establish and to receive believers into that kingdom.

In Matthew 24 the Lord said that two would be in the field. One would be taken away in judgment and the other left to go into the kingdom. Two women would be grinding at the mill. One would be taken away in judgment and the other left to go into the kingdom. That is the separation that takes place at the judgment that Christ will execute at His second advent. There will be one in Israel taken away in judgment and another left to go into the kingdom.

At the conclusion of Matthew 25 a second great judgment is mentioned. It is the judgment of nations or the judgment of Gentiles. Verse 31 says this judgment will take place when Christ returns to earth: "When the Son of man shall come in his glory, and all the holy angels with him, then shall he sit upon the throne of his glory." At the time of His ascension, Christ was received up into glory, and He was seated at the right hand of the Father in heaven. Some who are not careful students of the Word tend to confuse these two things. They believe verse 31 refers to Christ's ascension, so they think Christ's enthronement was at the time of His ascension. But notice that these are two quite different events. "The throne of his glory" is the throne that was promised to David in 2 Samuel 7:16 where God appeared to David, made a covenant with him and said one of his sons should sit on David's throne and rule over his kingdom forever. That throne of David was occupied by a number of David's descendants until Nebuchadnezzar removed the last Davidic descendant from the throne. The throne was left unoccupied until Jesus Christ came as the Son of David. He offered Himself to Israel as a King to occupy that throne.

Had He been received by Israel as their King, He would have occupied David's throne and would have revealed God's glory from that throne. But Israel rejected Him. Thus God postponed Christ's ascent to the Davidic throne until the second advent, when this throne will be reestablished over Israel and Christ as a Davidic Son will mount the throne and reveal the glory of God's power and love for Israel, as well as God's faithfulness to His covenants and promises as He regathers Israel and fulfills the promises made to them. So, in verse 31, Christ is pictured as mounting the throne promised to David to which He and He alone had the right, and He shall sit on the throne of His glory. And then before Him shall be gathered all nations (v. 32). Now the word translated "nations" is the Greek word that is most frequently translated "Gentiles." It may refer to nations as nations, or it may refer to Gentiles as people distinct from Israel. It is in that latter sense the word ought to be understood in verse 32: "Before him shall be gathered all the Gentiles."

In verses 1-30 Matthew has described Christ's judgment on Israel in which He separates the wise from the foolish, takes the wise into His kingdom and excludes the foolish. Now Matthew proceeds to the second aspect of this judgment at the second advent: judgment on Gentiles as Gentiles. According to Revelation 11:15 when Christ comes the second time, He will subdue nations as nations, and bring them under His authority: "The kingdoms of this world are become the kingdoms of our Lord, and of his Christ; and he shall reign for ever and ever." At the second event Christ will exert authority over nations as nations and subdue them and subjugate them to His authority. This is described in Revelation 19:15 where John says about the rider on the white horse:

> And out of his mouth goeth a sharp sword, that with it he should smite the nations: and he shall rule them with a rod of iron.

This again describes Christ's dealing with nations as nations, when at His second advent He will deal with every military alliance that has been aligned against Him. He will break the power of nations and will exert His authority over all who have called themselves kings and lords so that He shall be King of kings and Lord of lords. Thus at the second advent Christ will deal with nations as nations. This was described earlier in the studies of the campaign of Armageddon. But in Matthew 25:32 quite a different event in the prophetic program is described. While military powers will be broken and brought into subjection to Christ, multitudes of individual Gentiles will not be judged when armies are destroyed and military might is broken. And in order to determine who from among the Gentiles will enter into Christ's earthly millennial kingdom, there must be a judgment in which these Gentiles are judged concerning their salvation, concerning their faith in Jesus Christ. So it is for this point that Christ will gather all nations before Him.

From the time that God called Abraham, He had a purpose for Israel. But He also revealed to Abraham that He had a purpose for Gentile people. While Israel was the channel of blessing, Gentiles were to be blessed. In Genesis 12:3, for instance, God said to Abraham, "In thee [and in thy seed] shall all families of the earth be blessed." The Gentile peoples will be summoned before the throne of Christ's glory—the throne from which He manifests His essential glory and the glory of the Father. And when they gather there, they will be divided into two groups, sheep and goats. "He shall separate them one from another, as a shepherd divideth his sheep from the goats" (Mt 25:32). As far as Matthew records the incident here, there is not a word spoken. But a shepherd controls his sheep by the movements of his hands; if one of his flock gets stubborn or rebellious or refuses to obey the signals from his hand, then he brings his rod and his staff into play. Here Christ as shepherd of the flock is doing the shepherd's work and, with a motion, He separates sheep from goats, putting the sheep on His right hand and the goats on His left hand.

Following Oriental custom, the right hand is the place of privilege, of blessing, and the left hand was the place of separation. When Jacob wanted to bless his two grandsons, Ephraim and Manasseh, he was careful about which hand he placed on which son because their destiny would be determined by which hand was placed on them. Why? Because the right hand indicated the heir and, if he had put his right hand on Manasseh, he would have been elevated to the position of prominence and Ephraim would have been relegated to the inferior place. So he carefully placed his hands, crossing them to put the right hand on the right son.

The right hand was the place of privilege, the place of blessing, and there were those who were put on the right hand and others relegated to the position on His left hand. Christ then spoke to those on His right hand, and made a joyous announcement: "Come, ye blessed of my Father, inherit the kingdom prepared for you from the foundation of the world" (Mt 25:34).

It is interesting that Scripture should mention a kingdom prepared from the foundation of the world. God made a promise to Abraham in Genesis 12, long after the creation of the world. But that was not the beginning of God's program. At the outset God created this world to be a stage on which He would play out a great drama. It was to be a battlefield in which the contest between God and Satan would be fought out, and God had determined that when His adversary had been destroyed through the death of His Son, this battlefield would be transformed and made into a paradise where He would bring those who had believed Him and had trusted Him. There before the foundation of the world, in order to answer Satan's challenge that God had no right to be worshiped and believed and obeyed, God prepared a place and determined to populate it with those who had believed Him. So to those on His right hand He said, "Come ye blessed of my

Father, inherit the kingdom that God had prepared for you before this world was ever brought into existence." This is a triumphant note.

While it is a blessed invitation, some things about it created consternation, for Christ said to those invited into His kingdom,

> For I was an hungred, and ye gave me meat: I was thirsty, and ye gave me drink: I was a stranger, and ye took me in: naked, and ye clothed me: I was sick, and ye visited me: I was in prison, and ye came unto me (Mt 25:36).

To a casual reader, this may seem to be salvation by works, as though these people were received into Christ's kingdom because of what they had done. This passage is being used today to exhort and motivate people to all sorts of social action. It is the basis of the so-called Social Gospel that is being revived and preached today in which multitudes view the work of the church as the work of transforming society rather than redeeming individuals through Christ's death. They say that this verse proves that God accepts into His kingdom on the basis of what was done in the poverty program and in the welfare programs and the health programs. As a church you ought to be involved in that sort of thing. What a misunderstanding of the Scriptures to proceed on such a basis as that! What is our Lord teaching? The righteous do not understand what they have done for Him. Christ said, "Inasmuch as ye have done it unto one of the least of these my brethren, ye have done it unto me." (v. 40).

In order to understand what Christ is teaching, several other scriptures must be considered. Remember that following the church's rapture at the beginning of the tribulation period, God will sovereignly call and save 144,000 of the physical descendants of Abraham (Rev 7). Often referred to as the 144,000 witnesses, they will have the same ministry that the apostle Paul had in his day. They will go with the gospel of salvation by grace through faith to the ends of the earth.

They will tell men that Christ died and that there is salvation through His death, through His blood. As a result of their ministry, Revelation 7:14 says multitudes "washed their robes, and made them white in the blood of the Lamb." For the first three and one half years of the tribulation period, these witnesses will be privileged to preach without any interruption, with none to stop them. But then, according to Revelation 13, in the middle of the tribulation period, the head of the federated states of Europe will try to stifle the preaching of the gospel. He desires to exalt himself as God as well as king, and he forbids these to preach. Revelation says,

> It was given unto him to make war with the saints, to overcome them: and power was given him over all kindreds, and tongues, and nations. And all that dwell upon the earth shall worship him, whose names are not written in the book of life of the Lamb slain from the foundation of the world. And he causeth all, both small and great, rich and poor, free and bond, to receive a mark in their right hand, or in their foreheads: And that no man might buy or sell, save he that had the mark, or the name of the beast, or the number of his name (13:7, 16).

This head of the world government, which by that time will also have become head of the world church, will institute an economic system to control all men, and his edict will be that no man can buy food unless he has his ration card, his sign of submission to the authority of the government. Those who will have been going about as God's witnesses cannot and will not submit to his authority. They will refuse his identifying mark, not accepting his sign in their foreheads or on the palms of their hands. Therefore they will not be able to buy or sell. Even though they had independent wealth, they can't use it because they can't carry out the simplest business transaction without the sign of submission to the beast. As a result, they will go from place to place, hungry, destitute, pursued by the authority of the state, cast into prison, stripped of their clothing.

Although they will be in dire circumstances, they will keep on witnessing. What will sustain them? Their only sustenance will come from those who receive their message and believe in the Saviour they proclaim, and they will demonstrate that they have received the message of these messengers by providing for their physical and material needs. For example, a witness comes to a city and preaches. Somebody hears his message, and the Spirit bears witness with his spirit that this is the truth; and joyfully he receives Christ as Saviour. After the meeting, he goes to the messenger and says, "Where are you going to stay tonight?" The messenger replies, "I haven't the faintest idea. I can't go down to a motel. I don't have the proper ID card." And so the believer says, "Come home with me." But the witness says, "Don't you know that the powers that be have said that anyone who harbors one of us who preach the gospel will be persecuted for it?" He said, "Yes, but you also know that this same one has said that if you preach in the name of Christ, you are subject to a death penalty. You didn't stop. You brought the message to me, and I have salvation. You must come home with me." And he sets a meal before him, feeds him and clothes him. Someone tells the authorities that this witness has been disobeying the dictates of the government because he has been preaching.

During the night there comes a knock on the door, and the man is hauled into prison. The next morning this new believer comes to the prison with breakfast for the messenger. He nourishes him; he cares for him. Why? Because he has received the message that had been preached. That is the background of Christ's lesson in Matthew 25 where our Lord says to these whom He has invited into His kingdom, "Inasmuch as ye have done it unto one of the least of these my brethren [my witnesses], ye have done it unto me" (v. 40).

They were not saved because they fed, clothed, housed and visited one of God's servants, but they did these acts because they had been saved. This is not salvation by works, but their works bear evidence to their faith. This is what James is talking about when he says that faith without works is dead, barren or sterile. James is not teaching a man is saved by works, but he is showing that faith is a living thing and what is alive will reproduce itself. These have produced their works by faith, even with the threat of death hanging over them. They have ministered to God's minister. They are received into Christ's earthly millennial kingdom because of their faith in the message of salvation that was brought to them by these witnesses who are called "my brethren."

Then our Lord turns to the goats on His left hand and says, "Depart from me, ye cursed, into everlasting fire, prepared for the devil and his angels" (Mt 25:41). Why this curse? Why this judgment? He explains it in similar terms:

> For I was an hungred, and ye gave me no meat: I was thirsty, and ye gave me no drink: I was a stranger, and ye took me not in: naked, and ye clothed me not: sick, and in prison, and ye visited me not (v. 42).

They had had the same opportunity to hear and receive the message that the sheep had had, but they had demonstrated their rejection of the message by their lack of works. When they pleaded ignorance, Christ said, "Inasmuch as ye did it not to one of the least of these, ye did it not to me" (v. 45). Our Lord said in effect, "These ministers of mine came to you with an offer of salvation that would have washed you and made you white in the blood of the Lamb, but you rejected it. How do I know you rejected it? Because there was no fruit, no evidence of faith." Where there was no life, there can be no fruit; and if you sow chaff into the ground, you will never get a harvest. Where there is no life, there can be no fruit. So Christ uses their lack of works as a proof of their lack of faith, and they are excluded from His kingdom.

In verse 46 our Lord says, "And these shall go away into everlasting punishment." Those who have no faith in Christ, no faith in His salvation, who have rejected Him as personal Saviour, will go into everlasting punishment. But the righteous—those who have received Him and His salvation—will go into life eternal. To the Jewish mind, eternal life and entrance into the kingdom were synonymous terms. So our Lord was saying that when He comes He is coming as Judge and will determine just one question: "What have you done with the offer of salvation that I made for you? He will test all men's response to this offer of salvation. Those who have received it will be received into His kingdom. Those who have rejected it will be excluded from His kingdom. The issue is very clear; there is no middle ground. A man is either saved or he is lost. He is either in Christ, or he is out of Christ. He is either dead or he is alive. And when Jesus Christ comes the second time, before He manifests Himself as King over the earth, He will manifest Himself in His divine authority to judge man, to exclude the unbeliever, to receive the believers into His kingdom and to witness His glory.

God knows the facts and He knows that a man outside of Jesus Christ is forever lost. He is a sinner under divine judgment and must be separated from a holy and righteous God. Knowing all that and not being willing that any should perish, God sent His Son to save men from the very hell that men deny exists. Men hope they can deny it out of existence, but written in their hearts is the conviction that, as much as they wish it weren't so, it is so. That is why men fear death because, after death, said the writer to the Hebrews, is the certainty of judgment. God has given Jesus Christ the authority to judge men and has committed judgment to Him, and God's Son must make a just judgment in keeping with the facts. When a man is a sinner, there is only one just judgment: separation from God. The facts can't be altered. Any other judgment would be a perversion or miscarriage of justice. Christ came to offer men salvation and to offer Himself as Saviour so that men who trust Him might hear His word: "Come, ye blessed of my Father, inherit the kingdom prepared for you from the foundation of the world" (Mt 25:34).

17

THE GREAT SOCIETY–GOD'S OR MAN'S?

The pages of the Old Testament contain many graphic descriptions of the glory that shall come to this earth when Jesus Christ reigns as King of kings and Lord of lords. One of the major themes of the prophetic books is Christ's millennial kingdom. The prophets promised that the redeemed would live and reign with Him, and they waxed eloquent in their descriptions of the blessing, bounty and glory that should fill the earth when sin is restrained, when Satan is bound, when righteousness prevails, when Jesus Christ is King over all kings and Lord over all lords. From the time of the revelation of God through the prophets down through the ages of history, men have longed for just such a utopia as the prophets predicted. The Greek philosophers devoted a good deal of time to descriptions of the blessings that would cover the earth when all men entered into their knowledge and wisdom. They trusted that by wisdom they would introduce just such a utopia as the Word of God predicts. The theologian Augustine wrote a volume, *The City of God,* in which he described the glory that would belong to the earth when God's law is recognized and God's Son is crowned as King on this earth. Calvin, by establishing a theocracy in Geneva, hoped that he would see in his day just such a kingdom established on the earth as the prophets had predicted. Men have desired the fulfillment of that which the prophets have predicted, but they have not sought it in God's way, nor have they based their hopes for a transformed society in keeping with the revelation of Scripture.

In political, economic, social, educational and cultural spheres, the United States government has set a goal and outlined a program by which they are seeking to introduce into this country the "Great Society." They envision a society in which all inequities are abolished, injustice banished, and lawlessness done away. Poverty becomes a thing of the past. Sickness and disease have been curbed. Education meets the needs of men and raises them to a higher status, and there are no inequities between labor and management. These are all part of the programs of the great new society.

What is striking to a student of the Word of God is that these which seem to be such advanced programs in the thinking of our politicians are actually programs that God envisioned generations ago to be accomplished through Christ. Scripture can speak for itself because such a large volume of it is devoted to this subject. Certain passages will illustrate that God has a great society planned for this earth and for those who are received into the kingdom which Christ shall establish here.

One major problem confronting man's great society is the problem of war. How are we to solve the cold war as we look toward Europe, or to solve the hot war as we look toward the Orient? Midnight oil burns night after night as those in authority seek to cope with this problem. In order to try to establish peace on the earth, international organizations such as the United Nations have been formed. Men have been dispatched all over the world on so-called "peace-keeping missions." It is an anomaly to call the wars that we are fighting "peace-keeping missions." We are multiplying expenditures for armaments, spending untold billions in research to discover new weapons and in developing military power that can be ready at a moment's notice to move to any place on the face of the earth. That is man's solution to the problem of war. We hope that by building greater armies and more destructive weapons, we can dissuade our adversary from attacking us lest there should be retaliation in kind.

How different that is from the picture that the Word of God gives of the state of society when Christ shall return. For instance, Isaiah says, in describing the person and work of the coming King, that "His name shall be called Wonderful, Counsellor, The mighty God, The everlasting Father, The Prince of Peace. Of the increase of his government and peace there shall be no end, upon the throne of David, and upon his kingdom, to order it, and to establish it with judgment and with justice from henceforth even for ever" (9:6-7). When Christ was in a storm on the Sea of Galilee, He spoke peace to the sea, and there was a great calm. In coming to earth as a victorious general, He will speak peace to the nations, and the nations that are enmeshed in war will learn war no more. God's answer to the problem of war in the great society is not to build bigger or more numerous weapons, nor to summon larger armies, but to send Christ, the Prince of Peace, into this world. He will speak peace to the nations, and the nations that are like the troubled sea when it cannot rest and whose waters cast up dirt and mire, shall suddenly be at rest.

Another area that faces the great society is lawlessness. Lawlessness has spread abroad across the face of the land so that it is to be seriously questioned whether there has been a more lawless people than we are today. Having abandoned all standards of the Word of God, and having abandoned respect for law and law-enforcement agencies, we have become characterized as a lawless people. Consequently, our government has appropriated millions of dollars to study the problems of crime and lawlessness, and how the government may cope with these problems. How futile it is to seek to control men by some external means when the cause is internal, not external. When men are lawless externally it is because of rebelliousness against God and God's standard internally. One who would institute a great society in the United States must be able to handle the problem of lawlessness within our nation. But the Word of God shows that God has his answer to the problem of lawlessness. It is not to multiply law-enforcement agencies, nor is it to spend millions on investigating the causes of crime. It is to send Christ into this world. For instance, Micah the prophet writes:

> And many nations shall come, and say, Come, and let us go up to the mountain of the LORD, and to the house of the God of Jacob; and he will teach us of his ways, and we will walk in his paths: for the law shall go forth of Zion, and the word of the LORD from Jerusalem (Mic 4:2).

And Isaiah says,

> Thy people also shall be all righteous: they shall inherit the land for ever, the branch of my planting, the work of my hands, that I may be glorified (Is 60:21).

But the prophet gives another picture:

> But with righteousness shall he judge the poor, and reprove with equity for the meek of the earth: and he shall smite the earth with the rod of his mouth, and with the breath of his lips shall he slay the wicked (Is 11:4).

The one who will bring peace to the nations will do that which Micah predicts in Micah 4:3. He will cause the nations to beat their swords into plowshares and their spears into pruning hooks. He will not only bring peace between nations, but peace among individuals, for He is the law-giver. He is the one who has the right to judge, and His way shall be known, and men shall walk in it. His people shall be righteous. The Lord Jesus at the time of His reign will not only smite the wicked with the rod of His mouth so that transgressors will be removed from His kingdom, He will change the heart of men so that those who were once rebels will delight to walk in obedience to the law of God as it flows from the lips of the Lord Jesus Christ.

Another major problem that the leaders in our great society today face is injustice. This is a problem to which men give much attention. The arm of the Justice Department reaches further and further into many areas of our society because it is recognized that we cannot have a new and great society until injustices are removed, because where injustice exists there cannot be a great society. But it is not through the extension of the Justice Department that the new society will be instituted, for Isaiah gives God's solution to injustice:

> Behold my servant, whom I uphold; mine elect, in whom my soul delighteth; I have put my spirit upon him: he shall bring forth judgment to the Gentiles (42:1).

The Gentiles were the despised, the rejected, the downtrodden ones, those from whom blessings had been withheld. How would those for whom there was no justice receive justice? It would be through the coming of the Messiah, God's Servant. He will bring forth judgment to the Gentiles.

> He shall not cry, nor lift up, nor cause his voice to be heard in the street. A bruised reed shall he not break, and the smoking flax shall he not quench: he shall bring forth judgment unto truth. He shall not fail nor be discouraged, till he have set judgment in the earth: and the isles shall wait for his law (vv. 2-4).

Three times in those four verses the prophet establishes the fact that when God's Servant, the Lord Jesus, shall come He shall bring a just judgment to all men on the face of the earth, not only to the privileged ones but to the underprivileged, to those who are excluded. His judgment, according to verse 3, shall be in conformity to truth. God's answer to the problems of justice in the new society is not through the proliferation of the agents of the Justice Department, but to send a just one who will administer justice in keeping with the truth of the Word of God.

Another problem that the great society faces is ignorance. While we are one of the most literate nations on the face of the earth, in many respects we are one of the most ignorant nations, for knowledge that does not transform life is not true knowledge. We know a great deal about a great many things, but little about that which transforms life or character. In order to establish this new society on the earth, we multiply aid to education, as though by building better school systems we could change men. True education and true knowledge are based on the Word of God, for the fear of the Lord is the beginning of wisdom. When by the interpretations of our Supreme Courts we outlaw religion and any religious observance from our schools, we are removing the very foundation for wisdom from those for whom we are pouring millions and millions of dollars into the educational system. And those in positions of authority are ignorant of the fact that the Word of God is the foundation of wisdom. It is the foundation of knowledge. It is the foundation of all the liberty that we enjoy in this country.

But God has an answer to the problem of ignorance in His great society:

> They shall not hurt nor destroy in all my holy mountain: for the earth shall be full of the knowledge of the LORD, as the waters cover the sea. And though the Lord give you the bread of adversity, and the water of affliction, yet shall not thy teachers be removed into a corner any more, but thine eyes shall see thy teachers: and thine ears shall hear a word behind thee, saying, This is the way, walk ye in it, when ye turn to the right hand, and when ye turn to the left (Is 11:9; 30:20-21).

Habakkuk speaks again of the dissemination of knowledge through the personal appearance of the Lord Jesus Christ: "The earth shall be filled with the knowledge of the glory of the LORD, as the waters cover the sea" (2:14). These are but a few of many passages that deal with this important subject. As great as are our means of disseminating knowledge and communicating truth today, they are impotent to transform society by education alone. But God will send His Son who is the Revealer of God, who will lay a foundation for knowledge by revealing God to men. Then, on that revelation, He will build a new society that has at its foundation the knowledge of the Lord that shall cover the earth as the waters cover the sea.

Another problem in which our great society today has involved itself is sickness and disease. We are supporting medical research with untold millions in order to assist those who have been stricken. We have provided Medicare, and from the cradle to the grave we have insurance to take care of the physical needs of man. Yet disease still claims lives and removes people from the face of the earth. We do not for one moment minimize the benefits of the research done to discover the cause and the cure for disease. But in spite of all the medical research and all of the benefits that have come from it, that will not be God's answer to the problem of sickness and disease in His great society. Isaiah says,

> And the inhabitant shall not say, I am sick: the people that dwell therein shall be forgiven their iniquity. Then the eyes of the blind shall be opened, and the ears of the deaf shall be unstopped. Then shall the lame man leap as an hart, and the tongue of the dumb sing (Is 33:24; 35:5).

Why? Because Jesus Christ who created these bodies will be the Sustainer of these bodies when men come into His kingdom, and sickness and disease will be banished; He who touched the eyes of the blind and who raised the dead when He walked among men will minister to the physical needs of men. Jeremiah speaks of this same truth:

> For I will restore health unto thee, and I will heal thee of thy wounds, saith the LORD; because they called thee an Outcast, saying, This is Zion, whom no man seeketh after (Jer 30:17).

While the prophet is speaking there of the restoration of the city of Jerusalem, he is stating a principle: When Jesus Christ comes He will be the Restorer and Sustainer of physical bodies during the time of His earthly reign.

In connection with this, another problem men face in the great society is the rehabilitation of those who have been stricken or incapacitated in some way. Again, we would not for one moment minimize the beneficial effects of this type of research and this work, yet we find that this is not the ultimate answer. As is evident in Isaiah 35, God will not establish rehabilitation centers for the weak and the maimed and the lame, nor lighthouses for the blind. He will remove the cause, not deal with the symptoms. That is God's answer to the medical problem of the great society.

Another problem that the great society has to face is the problem of oppression by legislation. Our government has sought to solve the problem of civil rights, one of the great social problems which would prevent the institution of the great society here in our country. Yet we find that God has another and a better answer. It's not through legislation; it's not through civil rights movements; it's not through advocating civil disobedience to remove oppression for the oppressed. There is a need for a deliverer, and Isaiah describes His coming:

> I the LORD have called thee in righteousness, and will hold thine hand, and will keep thee, and give thee for a covenant of the people, for a light of the Gentiles (42:6).

Again, the Gentiles were the unprivileged peoples of the prophet's day, and the Messiah was to come to do something for the unprivileged. He would

> open the blind eyes, to bring out the prisoners from the prison, and them that sit in darkness out of the prison house. I am the LORD: that is my name: and my glory will I not give to another, neither my praise to graven images (v. 7).

The prophet also writes:

> And it shall come to pass in the day that the LORD shall

> give thee rest from thy sorrow, and from thy fear, and from the hard bondage wherein thou wast made to serve, that thou shalt take up this proverb against the king of Babylon, and say, How hath the oppressor ceased! The golden city ceased! The LORD hath broken the staff of the wicked, and the sceptre of the rulers (Is 14:3-5).

In those verses Isaiah is anticipating the work of God's Deliverer who will set the captives free, who will deliver the oppressed from their oppression, and deal with the oppressors who held them in subservience. God's answer to the problem of oppression is not legislation; it is not to institute more marches; it is to send a Deliverer to institute His new society.

Another major problem that those in authority today would like to ignore or sidestep is the problem between labor and management. No problem is more plaguing to those in authority today than how to settle disputes between labor and management, how to ward off strikes that threaten to cripple the nation. They set up labor mediation boards. They have laws in order to try to handle these problems. But these are incapable of introducing a new society in the area of labor-management relations. The Word of God also has something to say about that:

> The LORD hath sworn by his right hand, and by the arm of his strength, Surely I will no more give thy corn to be meat for thine enemies; and the sons of the stranger shall not drink thy wine, for the which thou hast laboured: but they that have gathered it shall eat it, and praise the LORD; and they that have brought it together shall drink it in the courts of my holiness. And they shall build houses, and inhabit them; and they shall plant vineyards, and eat the fruit of them. They shall not build, and another inhabit; they shall not plant, and another eat: for as the days of a tree are the days of my people, and mine elect shall long enjoy the work of their hands. They shall not labour in vain, nor bring forth for trouble; for they are the seed of the blessed of the LORD, and their offspring with them (Is 62:8-9; 65:21-23).

In these passages the prophet is describing an equitable social structure in which one does not labor and then another receive the benefits of his labor. He describes such an equitable distribution of materials and labor that there shall be abundance for all. No labor mediation board can do that which the Lord Jesus Christ will do at His coming, for He will institute such a just and equitable society that the conflict between labor and management that results from selfishness on both sides will cease. Society will become equitable because Christ will be a just administrator, and the prophets anticipate the solution to the problems existing between labor and management through Christ's coming. The farm problem has been plaguing Washington officials ever since the time when they began to plow pigs under the earth in the Depression years to keep the price of pork high. There seems to be no solution, for when the earth ought to be withholding its bounty to keep prices up, the earth produces in spite of all that Washington wants it to do. A rigged economy in Washington is no answer to the problems of the great society in the area of the earth's productivity. Amos has something to say about that:

> Behold, the days come, saith the Lord, that the plowman shall overtake the reaper, and the treader of grapes him that soweth seed; and the mountains shall drop sweet wine, and all the hills shall melt. And I will bring again the captivity of my people of Israel, and they shall build the waste cities, and inhabit them; and they shall plant vineyards, and drink the wine thereof; they shall also make gardens, and eat the fruit of them (9:13-14).

While many today are afraid of starvation on a wide scale because of the overproduction of the world's population, God envisions a time when there will be bounty for all in face of spiraling population explosion, because God will send material bounty that will meet man's needs. It will not be periods when the barns will be full for some and the coffers empty for others, when one of the pressing problems will be the problem of poverty and starvation. The prophet reveals that there will be an economy in which cities will be built to house the multitudes that will be born, and the earth will produce bountifully to feed the population of the earth because God the Creator is the Provider, and there will be no withholding of the benefits of the earth by His hand.

Related to this is the problem of prosperity. Our government seeks to bring in a new society by the Anti-Poverty Program, and by the distribution of wealth particularly to the so-called "underprivileged." They seek to introduce a minimum wage which will deliver men from the burden of poverty. Is that the answer? Look again in the prophets:

> Then shall he give the rain of thy seed, that thou shalt sow the ground withal; and bread of the increase of the earth, and it shall be fat and plenteous; in that day shall thy cattle feed in large pastures. The oxen likewise and the young asses that ear the ground shall eat clean provender, which hath been winnowed with the shovel and with the fan (Is 30:23-24).

Ezekiel speaks of the bounty and plenty of God's provision for all men:

> And I will make them and the places round about my hill a blessing; and I will cause the shower to come down in his season; there shall be showers of blessing. And the tree of the field shall yield her fruit, and the earth shall yield her increase, and they shall be safe in their land, and shall know that I am the LORD. I will also save you from all your uncleannesses: and I will call for the corn, and will increase it, and lay no famine upon you. And I will multiply the fruit of the tree, and the increase of the field, that ye shall receive no more reproach of famine among the heathen (34:26-27; 36:29-30).

In these and many other passages the prophets promise that when Christ reigns, He will solve the problems of hunger, famine, prosperity, or economic need by providing abundantly for all those that have subjected themselves to His authority.

One of the great problems about which our great society seems little concerned is the problem of godlessness. This, of course, is coupled with the problem of lawlessness that goes to the very heart of the needs of men. No government can instill a fear of God, a knowledge of God, or a love for God in the hearts of its people. But when Christ comes to introduce God's society, He will bring the fear of the Lord into the hearts of those whom He receives into His kingdom. Zechariah speaks of this:

> Thus saith the LORD of hosts; In those days it shall come to pass, that ten men shall take hold of all languages of the nations, even shall take hold of the skirt of him that is a Jew, saying, We will go with you: for we have heard that God is with you (8:23).

The nation Israel, that was set as a light to the world, will function as a light and bring men a knowledge of God so that they shall trust Him. Zechariah says:

> And it shall come to pass in that day, saith the LORD of hosts, that I will cut off the names of the idols out of the land, and they shall no more be remembered: and also I will cause the prophets and the unclean spirit to pass out of the land (13:2).

All idolatry will be removed when the Lord Jesus reigns. Zechariah gives an interesting picture in the closing verses of his prophecy:

> In that day shall there be upon the bells of the horses, HOLINESS UNTO THE LORD; and the pots in the LORD's house shall be like the bowls before the altar (14:20).

What Zechariah is saying is that in that day there will be no division into secular and sacred so that one part of a man's life is within this world and another part of his life is lived with God. He says that when horses go down the street and the bells of their harnesses jingle, the melody they make will be a melody of praise unto the Lord, "Holiness unto the Lord." And every pot in the kitchen of the home will be set apart to the Lord as much as the vessels that were dedicated to God in the temple. His picture is that of a great new society that is completely under the authority of the King of kings and Lord of lords, of people who worship, serve, love and obey Him, a people whose needs are completely met through the Deliverer. He is the Healer. He is the Provider. He is the Redeemer.

Many of the problems that we think of as being uniquely our problems in this day are problems for which God has a solution and has offered us a solution in the person of Jesus Christ. What a tragedy that a nation that calls itself Christian should ignore God's solution to men's social, economic, political and religious problems and seek to substitute the devices of men for the plan of God. But God, who knows the needs of man, purposes through Jesus Christ to satisfy every need. Our government will never bring us into the great society. Only the Son of God, who comes in power and great glory, can meet the needs of men and nations. Through His own return He will institute a great new society on this earth.

18

WHAT WILL WE DO IN HEAVEN?

MOST BELIEVERS have a very nebulous concept of heaven. Perhaps it is because none of us has yet been there, nor have we talked with any traveler who has gone with a camera and shown slides on his return. Much of our concept of heaven has been fashioned either by cartoonists or by hymnologists, both of whom are generally wrong when it comes to the scriptural concept of heaven. The hymnologist thinks of heaven as a place where believers sit under the shade of a tree with a soft breeze blowing upon them to keep them cool as they relax day after day. The prospect seems monotonous. The cartoonist pictures the saint sitting on the edge of a cloud with his feet hanging over into nothingness, about to slip off into space; and while it might seem exciting to float on a cloud, the prospect presents little that would interest after the novelty had worn off.

It is strange that the Bible says so little about heaven. But if God fully revealed to us the splendors and glories of heaven, we would never again be satisfied to live out our appointed span of years here. If we don't know much about what heaven looks like, or much about the surroundings or circumstances, the Bible seems to have even less to say about what we will be doing for eternity; and an eternity with nothing to do is a rather frightening anticipation. Yet, some hints are given. No specific chapters spell out in detail exactly what we will be doing in heaven, but a few scattered words or phrases of Scripture seem to give some suggestions as to how we will be occupied throughout eternity. Hopefully these glimpses will create an appetite to be absent from the body and present with the Lord, to be home in glory with Him.

The four areas that we will cover are those of worship, instruction, fellowship and service. First of all when we see our Lord face to face, when we have been brought in a redeemed, glorified body and are at home in His presence, we will be occupied in worship. John writes,

> And I heard a great voice out of heaven saying, Behold, the tabernacle of God is with men, and he will dwell with them, and they shall be his people, and God himself shall be with them, and be their God (Rev 21:3).

In this passage John is thinking back to an Old Testament truth. God had appointed a meeting place between Himself and the nation Israel in the tabernacle. The plan of the tabernacle was revealed to Moses when he was in the mount, and all of the sacrifices and the worship carried on in the tabernacle were a matter of divine revelation. When God revealed the plan of the tabernacle, He said to Moses, "There will I meet with you." The tabernacle was designed to be a meeting place between God and man. Men could approach God through blood sacrifice. That is why the prominence was given to the altar and the sacrifices which would be offered upon the altar. Only those who had been cleansed could come into the presence of God. Those who come to God are to come with their offerings, prayers, and worship. The altar of incense was a revelation concerning worship. Those who came to God were to feed upon the Word of God. Hence the table of shewbread. Those who had been redeemed by blood and cleansed by the washing of the water with the Word were to be lights to the world. This is suggested in the lampstand. Everything in the tabernacle was looking toward the presence of God, which was revealed through the shining of light that was above the mercy seat on the ark in the holy of holies. All that was in the tabernacle was designed to bring a sinner into the presence of God as a redeemed worshiper. "There will I meet with you."

Turning from the past to the future, John says that things of which the tabernacle was only a foreshadowing would be realized, and that God would dwell with man, and man would have access to God. Man would dwell in His presence and for what purpose? That in eternity man might realize that of which the tabernacle in the wilderness was ony a foreshadowing, that those who had been redeemed and cleansed might become a worshiping people. God says, "Whoso offereth praise glorifieth me" (Ps 50:23). The writer to the Hebrews in chapter 13 says that even in the new age there are certain sacrifices which God desires—the sacrifices were not bloody sacrifices of lambs and goats and bullocks, because the sacrifice of Christ was sufficient; but the sacrifices that God desired were the sacrifices of worship and praise, even the fruit of our lips, giving thanks to His name. The one who worships God recognizes the splendor and the perfection of the character of God, and the one who offers thanksgiving recognizes the gifts that God has given to man. And throughout all eternity believers will be occupied primarily with giving worship and praise and thanksgiving to God because of what He is, because of His sovereign position over all creation. Things in heaven, and things in earth, and things under the earth shall bow before Him and give honor and glory to Him. It will be the delight of God's children collectively and individually to dwell with Him and to worship Him. They are a worshiping people because of what God is, because of what He has done.

In the Old Testament there was a barrier between the worshiper and God. That barrier was the veil, and only the high priest could go behind the veil. Even he could not go in without blood, in order that he might offer an offering of blood upon the mercy seat to God. In the New Testament the veil that kept men from God was the body of Jesus Christ. God was in Christ revealing Himself and reconciling the world to Himself, but men could know God only through

Christ and had to come to God through Jesus Christ. In the eternal state every veil will be taken away because the barrier of sin will be completely and perfectly removed, and we will come into the presence of God and will dwell with Him. We will be His people. God Himself shall be with us and be our God. First of all in heaven, then, we will be worshipers.

In the second place, in the eternal state we will be students. Paul writes,

> When I was a child, I spake as a child, I understood as a child, I thought as a child: but when I became a man, I put away childish things. For now we see through a glass, darkly; but then face to face: now I know in part; but then shall I know even as also I am known (1 Co 13:11-12).

Eternity will be spent not only in worshiping God but also in the pursuit of a knowledge of God. The Old Testament was God's revelation to man, and what men in that day knew of God they knew through that revelation. A man like David who walked with God and who communed with Him upon his bed at night learned what he learned of God by searching the Scriptures, because the Scriptures were God's revelation to man. That is why David could say that they were his meat night and day.

When Jesus Christ came, He came not to do away with the Old Testament scriptures, but to add to them further revelation concerning God. In John 1, Christ made it very clear that no man knows God except the Son who came from the bosom of the Father, and that Son has revealed the Father to man. What we know of God today we know through the Scriptures and through the Son. But God is not a God who could possibly be contained in the pages of a book. John refers to that fact when he, even in speaking of the revelation made during the earthly life of Christ, says all of the libraries of the world could not contain the volumes that could be written.

But Jesus Christ did not fully reveal God, for men could

not comprehend that revelation. Yet, it is God's nature to reveal Himself; He takes no delight in hiding Himself away or being unknown. Because we have such a limited capacity and finite minds, we can comprehend little of an infinite God. When we get to glory and the limitations of the flesh and the limitations imposed on our perception by sin have all been taken away, God will reveal and disclose Himself. A finite God could reveal Himself totally and completely in a limited amount of time, but an infinite God may require all eternity to reveal Himself. So what are we going to spend eternity doing? No doubt we will be receiving new revelation as an infinite God adds to what has already been disclosed by further revelation so that we might know Him.

What was the great consuming passion of the apostle Paul? In Philippians 3:10 he said, "That I may know him." When you read the epistles you conclude that Paul knew more about Jesus Christ and God than any other man. All Bible students and theologians since Paul's day have only been trying to understand what Paul himself knew, but no theologian adds anything to the revelation already disclosed. But with all that Paul had had revealed to him, he still knew only an infinitesimal part of what is to be known about God. But we shall receive expanded knowledge when God reveals Himself and when He gives to His redeemed, glorified saints the capacity to understand Him. We are not infinite now and never will be. Therefore, God can never reveal Himself all at once to us. So God little by little will add to our understanding of Himself. I think that is what Paul had in mind when he said in 1 Corinthians 13: "For now we see through a glass dimly; but then face to face." John writes in Revelation 21:4,

> And God shall wipe away all tears from their eyes; and there shall be no more death, neither sorrow, nor crying, neither shall there be any more pain: for the former things are passed away.

Throughout eternity we will receive by revelation not only a knowledge of God but a knowledge of His dealing with us. So many things come into our experience today that we simply do not understand and for which there is no explanation; but God will not leave those riddles unsolved. He will wipe away tears from our eyes by explaining the mystery of His will. He will show us how He worked and why He permitted us to go through certain experiences.

Recently I received a call from a brokenhearted father who with his wife and children had been attending our services for some time. They told me that their seven-year-old boy had been struck by a hit-and-run driver and had been killed, and asked if I would have the service. I went into that home to talk with them and to pray with them. The mother said in the course of our conversation, "We can't understand it, and we know you can't explain it; but we believe that God makes no mistakes. Someday we'll understand." Those heartbroken parents would like to know why, and someday they will know because probably a part of eternity will be spent in listening as God explains to us why things happened and how things worked together for good.

The sorrows, heartaches and burdens that we bore will all be lifted, and that will be a part of our learning process. Eternity is to be spent in receiving revelation concerning God and the mystery of God's dealings, the wonder of His will. What a joy it will be to have this unfolding. If you can speak of eternity in terms of days and years, every passing day of eternity will bring a new revelation of the glory, splendor and majesty of God. Knowledge begets love, so the more we know of Him, the more we will love Him. He reveals Himself not simply to satisfy intellectual curiosity, but He reveals Himself and explains His working so that our love might be an increasing love for Him for the unending ages of eternity.

The third thing with which we will be occupied in eternity is fellowship. There are two aspects of this we would like to call to your attention. In Revelation 22:4, in describing the millennial age and Christ's relationship to millennial saints, John writes, "They shall see his face." This suggests the idea of a personal, intimate fellowship between the child of God and the Lord Jesus Christ. Fellowship is the response of the mind, heart and will of the child of God to the mind, heart and will of Christ. It will be our privilege to enter into the fullness of fellowship. We will give our redeemed minds to the truth of God and purified hearts to the love of Christ, our wills to obey Him perfectly and implicitly through the unending ages of eternity. When our Lord first chose the Twelve, as recorded in Mark 3:14, He chose them "that they should be with him." The primary purpose in selecting the Twelve was to provide fellowship for the heart of Christ and then that they might respond to His fellowship. That for which the Twelve were called when Christ walked on earth will be the privilege of every child of God. "We shall see His face."

When we are at home with the Lord, there will be no obstacles, barriers or shut doors, but personal, open communion between the Son of God and the child of God. It will be our delight to go into His presence and to experience what Mary did as she sat at His feet and heard His Word. She communed with Him, and that will be our delight and our privilege. But not only will we be occupied with fellowship with Christ, we will also be occupied in fellowship with other believers. In 1 Corinthians 13:12, Paul says, "Then shall I know even as also I am known." This speaks not only of fellowship vertically between the believer and Christ, but also fellowship horizontally between a believer and other believers.

One of the joys of a pastor is meeting with those saints whose desire it is to become a part of the fellowship of the church. One question that we are interested in is how that person came to know Jesus Christ as his own personal Saviour. So when people come before our board, we ask them to tell how this happened. I wish that sometimes you could be there to hear these testimonies. Every one is different. But it is a joy each time we hear a testimony of salvation. I don't know how many saints are going to be in glory, but everyone who will be there is a miracle of God's grace. I know I will not be satisfied until I have had an opportunity to hear each saint recite how he came to know Jesus Christ as personal Saviour. It will be the most thrilling thing to hear the saints recount the marvel of God's grace. We will fellowship with Him, and with one another. Fellowship depends on knowledge. We don't have real fellowship together because we don't know each other. Somehow we never seem to have time enough to get to know each other here, but there we will. You see, this is a part of our fellowship together—getting to know one another. We don't know Abraham. We don't know David. We don't know Elijah. We don't know Zechariah. We don't know Peter or Paul. But someday we will know them. The only way we will know them is to sit down and spend time with them, and we will have lots of it. It will be our delight to spend time in fellowship together, recounting the goodness of God's grace and knowing one another as members of the family of God.

A clue to the fourth thing we will do in eternity is found in Revelation 22:3: "His servants shall serve him." We live in bodies that grow weak, that get tired, that need sleep at night, that need rest and refreshment. When it says "there remaineth therefore a rest to the people of God," we somehow conceive of heaven as a place where there is a cessation of all activity. Rest is not cessation of activity, but a change of activity. During the summer vacation somebody asked me, "Are you having a good rest this summer?" I said, "I certainly am." They said, "What have you been doing?" I said, "I am painting my house." They replied, "You call that rest?" Yes, to me that is rest. Several years ago we took one of the fellows from the church up to a lake cottage with us. We told him that we were going up for a rest. We did what we usually do when we rest: we cut down trees, sawed them up for firewood, cleared brush and mowed the lawn. That fellow came back exhausted. He said at the end of the day, "You call this rest?" Yes, to me that is rest. It is not cessation of activity, but it is a change of activity. When we speak of heaven as a place of rest, it is not a place where nothing is done, for Scripture says His servants shall serve Him. God will have some work for every one of His children to do that will occupy them through the ages of eternity. I don't know what the work is. I don't know the nature of it, but I know that we will work. Work was not a curse put on man. Work was a blessing given by God to Adam in the garden before the fall. Before Adam sinned he was told that he was to dress or cultivate the garden. The curse added perspiration to his work, but work itself was not the result of the curse. For eternity we will be working, and will be occupied for Him. The word translated "serve" here is the same word that is used of the service of a priest in the temple, and it shows that no matter what work God assigns us to do in the management of His affairs throughout eternity, God will view it as a priestly ministry. It will be the worship and service that are rendered unto God by those who have been set apart to God. Each child of God will have a responsibility and will contribute something to the welfare of all the body of the redeemed. What you will be doing no other person can possibly do, and all the redeemed will be depending on you to do that thing.

That is how we will spend eternity: worshiping, learning, fellowshiping and working. All center in a person. It is He whom we worship. It is of Him we learn. It is with Him we fellowship, and it will be Him whom we serve. God gives us the privilege of a foretaste of heaven now, because we can worship now, we can learn of Him now, we can fellowship with Him now. We can serve now. That is why the hymn writer said,

> Blessed assurance,
> Jesus is mine.
> Oh, what a foretaste of glory divine.

19

WHAT WILL HEAVEN BE LIKE?

IN REVELATION 21–22 the apostle John gives a glimpse of what heaven will be like. It is impossible to fully comprehend a realm which we have never seen and it is difficult to translate heaven into earthly terms so we can understand. The glory of God's presence is so far beyond man's comprehension that when John tried to describe what was revealed to him, he has to describe it in terms of reflected sunlight and gleaming gems and glittering gold that has been polished to mirror brilliance. Ezekiel faced this same problem. In the first chapter of his prophecy the glory of God was revealed to him, and the dazzling brilliance of the Shekinah of God burst upon him. As he sought to describe what he saw, he could describe it only in terms of the sun shining on polished jewels. In Revelation 1, when the apostle John was given a revelation of the glory of the resurrected, glorified Christ, he spoke of the glory of that person in terms of sunlight shining upon new-fallen snow. Thus the Word of God attempts to describe the brilliance of the glory of God. Heaven, first of all, is the presence of God. This does not mean that heaven is not a place, for it certainly is; but heaven is more than that and when we think of heaven we have to think of it first of all as the place of God's revealed presence, where He displays His glory. In Revelation 22:4, John wrote concerning the redeemed: "They shall see his face." Christ in John 14:3 intimated the same truth when He said, "And if I go and prepare a place for you, I will come again, and receive you unto myself; that where I am, there ye may be also." The apostle Paul in 1 Thessalonians 4:16-17 says that the Lord Himself shall descend from heaven with a voice of the archangel with a shout and with the trump of God, and the living shall be caught up together with the resurrected in the clouds to meet the Lord in the air and so shall we ever be with the Lord. The Bible never refers to Christ coming to take us to heaven. It always refers to Christ coming to take us to Himself or to take us home to the Father, to take us into the Father's house. The concept of heaven in the Word of God is the concept of being in the presence of God the Father, God the Son, and God the Holy Spirit. When we realize that this is the concept of Scripture it makes the question so often asked, "Where is heaven?" of little importance. Do not try to fix heaven. Heaven is the presence of God.

When Christ was in conflict with the Pharisees, as recorded in Luke 20, they came to Him in order to discredit Him with a question for which they felt there was no answer. It was a puzzling question of the man who died whose brother took his widow and he died, and so on until all seven brothers had fulfilled the requirements of the Levitical law and had married their deceased brother's wife. The question asked was: In the resurrection which one of the brothers will claim her as his wife? The Lord said,

> The children of this world marry, and are given in marriage: but they which shall be accounted worthy to obtain that world, and the resurrection from the dead, neither marry, nor are given in marriage: Neither can they die any more: for they are equal [or they are like] unto the angels; and are the children of God, being the children of the resurrection (vv. 34-36).

We know that the unfallen angels dwell in the presence of God, and they are dispatched from His presence according to His will to fulfill His commands. The angels dwell in the presence of God, and the redeemed, Christ said, in resurrection are to be like angels. Now He is not speaking there primarily of their physical appearance. He is speaking of their place of residence.

Paul says in 1 Corinthians 15 that there are different kinds of bodies. On this earth there are different kinds of bodies, bodies of birds and fishes and man. He also tells us that there are bodies that are suited to existence on this earth, and there are bodies that are suited to existence in heaven. Angels are not disembodied spirits floating around like a wisp of cloud. Angels dwell in celestial bodies or a body suited for heaven, and they in these celestial bodies are in the presence of God. The resurrected, Christ taught in Luke 20:36, will be like angels in that they will dwell in celestial bodies in the presence of God.

In order to reveal something about heaven and about life in the presence of God, in Revelation 21–22 emphasis is put on the description of a city. In Revelation 21:10 John says that he was carried in the spirit to a great and high mountain and was showed that great city, the holy Jerusalem, descending out of heaven from God. John intended to convey a number of details about what heaven is like by referring to the abode of the redeemed in eternity as a city. The first city mentioned in the Word of God was the city founded by Nimrod (Gen 10) ; and its history is given in Genesis 11. Apparently before that time men had not lived in cities, but they joined together so that their rebellion against God would be organized. They came into the city of Babel so they might unite in their opposition to God and in their repudiation of His truth, and all of those who lived there were apostates and renegades. They realized that they would need defense, and so they congregated together in their unbelief. They could better declare themselves independent of God by uniting in their unbelief than they could continue in their rebellion as independent, isolated individuals.

Hebrews 12:22 reads: "But ye are come unto mount Sion, and unto the city of the living God, the heavenly Jerusalem." Notice the emphasis on the city again there. In this heavenly

Jerusalem there are several groups that are identifiable. First of all, he refers to "an innumerable company of angels" (v. 22). This would refer to all the unfallen angels who have faithfully served God from the time of their creation, having resisted the temptation of Lucifer who sought to draw all the angels after himself. This heavenly city will be occupied first of all by the unfallen angels. Second, he refers to the "general assembly and church of the first born" (v. 23*a*). We believe that this refers to the church of this present age, the church which is Christ's body, that body of which He is the head that began at Pentecost and continues until the rapture. This then is the second identifiable group, the church of this present age.

The third group is "the spirits of just men made perfect" (v. 23*b*). Evidently this refers to all Old Testament saints and the tribulation saints from the time of Adam down to the inception of the church on Pentecost and from the rapture to the second advent. It would also include all millennial saints, who were born and redeemed in the millennial age. This is a third, separate, identifiable group. The church and the spirits of just men—the Old Testament saints and the New Testament saints—comprise the total body of the redeemed. They are all there by faith through grace, based on the death of Christ; but they are there in a different relationship to Christ. The church is there as His bride. The Old Testament saints are there as the friends of the Bridegroom. They are related to Christ. They are within the body of the redeemed. God, the judge of all, is in the city (Heb 12:23) and "Jesus the mediator of the new covenant" (v. 24) will also be there. Thus, along with the unfallen angels, the Old Testament saints, and the church saints, the Father and the Son are present. The redeemed who occupy this heavenly city are together in the presence of God.

John describes this city in Revelation 21. First he says it has the "glory of God" (v. 11). John saw this city descending from heaven the same way the pillar of fire or the cloud descended from heaven and hovered over the tabernacle in the Old Testament. As it descended from heaven it displayed the glory of God. The city was glorious and, in order to describe it, he says her light was like unto a stone most precious, even like a jasper stone, clear as crystal (v. 11). Jasper is a diamond or a colorless stone that when polished radiates and reflects the light with dazzling brilliance. So when John wanted to describe the city's glory, he said it was like the light of the sun reflected in a diamond that blinds one. The city is not glorious because of the material things out of which it is built but because of the fact that God is personally present.

David collected gold, silver, timber and stones to build a temple in Jerusalem. Solomon constructed the temple. When it was dedicated, the Shekinah glory of God filled the temple, and the glory of the temple was not its gold and silver. It was the fact that God was there. The tabernacle in the wilderness was made of linen and animal skins, and after a time in the desert it probably was drab and dull, uninteresting to the sight; but when God moved into that tabernacle and filled it, then it was glorious—not because of the cunning work in the materials nor because of the skins that had been dyed—but because God was personally present.

John says in Revelation 21 that this city in which we will dwell is the home of all the redeemed, together with the unfallen angels who are in God's presence. The redeemed behold God's glory and, like little diamonds, they radiate and reflect God's glory because He is personally present with them. John is emphasizing not so much a place nor the materials out of which the city is made, as a relationship to a Person. That is why I like the hymn "The Sands of Time" because it emphasizes the fact that the Lamb is all the glory of Immanuel's land.

John also says this city is a protected place for it has a high wall with twelve gates (21:12). The ancient city wall was erected for the inhabitants' protection, with walls high enough to prevent any adversary from scaling them, and gates stout enough to keep any adversary from battering them down. A city was as safe as its gates and walls. In describing the place where we will dwell, John emphasizes that it is a protected city in which the inhabitants will live in perfect safety and security, without fear. He emphasizes that while this city has gates, they shall not "be shut at all by day: for there shall be no night there" (v. 25). What is the purpose of having gates if they are always open? John shows that the residents do not dwell in safety because of the physical gates, but they are in safety and peace because of the one in whose presence they dwell. While the emblems of security are there, they do not depend on them for security. Instead, they are depending on the one in whose presence they rest. So, heaven will be a place of rest, safety and security because the redeemed are in God's presence, and God's holiness sets bounds so that no unholy thing can approach. Were it possible for one to climb out of hell, he still could not enter into God's presence to defile or corrupt the city nor the saints because the holiness of God protects from all that would threaten.

The next thing John points out is that this city has twelve foundations (v. 14). The foundations emphasize the permanence of the city. When builders prepare to build a building, foundations are dug to solid rock, because when a building is founded upon rock, it is unshakeable and unmoveable. The building's permanence is inseparably tied with the foundation upon which it rests. This city is a permanent city because it has foundations. In the foundation are the names of the twelve apostles of the Lamb. Our Lord said to Peter, "Thou art Peter, and upon this rock [that is, on Myself] I will build my church" (Mt 16:18). Christ is the foundation. Paul told the Corinthians that "other foundation can no may lay than that which is laid, which is Christ Jesus" (1 Co 3:11). This city is founded upon the eternal rock, the Son of God, and He is not only its protective wall, He is its foundation, and our security depends upon that foundation.

Next we find that the city is a spacious city built on a

square, and the length is as large as the breadth. The measure of the city was 12,000 furlongs, which is approximately 1,500 miles. Some visualize this as a cube with four dimensions. Others view it as a pyramid with three dimensions, but the picture is the same . He is emphasizing spaciousness. Today 1,500 miles is not far, but Christ was born in Nazareth, thirty miles inland from the Mediterranean Sea and, as far as Scripture records, He never saw it once. He traveled the ninety miles from Galilee to Jerusalem, because He was compelled to attend the feasts. So when John spoke of a city 1,500 miles by 1,500 miles by 1,500 miles, he was speaking of that which was beyond comprehension. What was John trying to tell us? Not so much the physical dimensions of the city as he is the fact that it is a spacious city, that it is sufficient to bring all of the redeemed ones of God into the Father's presence.

The list of the twelve precious stones that adorn the city emphasizes the fact of the city's beauty. The beauty is not that the streets are of gold, although John says they are, nor that the gates are pearls, nor that the walls are decked with jewels. He describes these in order to convey the fact of an indescribable beauty. The beauty of God is His holiness. This city will reveal and reflect the beauty of holiness, and those who dwell in the city as holy ones will display and reflect the glory of God, the glory of His holiness. God's glory fills every part of the city and is manifest throughout, so that the entire place partakes of the glory of His holiness. When Zechariah closes his prophecy concerning the earthly reign of Christ, he says that all the pots, vessels and houses shall be holiness to the Lord, and even the bells of the horses going through the streets tinkle holiness to the Lord. He is showing us that God's character will permeate everything, and that the frying pan on the stove will partake of the character of God, reflect the beauty of the glory of God's holiness just as the tabernacle and the temple in the Old Testament were instruments to reflect the glory of God.

> And the city had no need of the sun, neither of the moon, to shine in it: for the glory of God did lighten it, and the Lamb is the light thereof (Rev 21:23).

In this city there is no darkness. God sent darkness to this earth to provide for man's physical rejuvenation, to provide an opportunity for rest and sleep. Man has invented floodlights so he can do what God never intended him to do—to work through the night. We need the rest of the night. But in that city there will be no need for night. Why? Because there is no weakness. There is no loss of strength. There is no need for rest because the body will not become tired and exhausted. The one who came as light into the world will cause His light to shine throughout the city so that men will walk in the light of His countenance. There will be no night there because we will walk in the light of His countenance. A child is never afraid of the sunshine; he is only afraid of the dark and shadows. He's not afraid of what is revealed in the daylight; he's afraid of what lurks in the shadows. When John says there is no night there, he is reminding us that God has removed every cause of fear, and He brings peace by His presence. So the city will be a fearless place.

A final thing is revealed:

> In the midst of the street of it, and on either side of the river, was there the tree of life, which bare twelve manner of fruits, and yielded her fruit every month: and the leaves of the tree were for the healing of the nations (22:2).

In order to understand the picture given here, this city must be conceived of as a pyramid rather than as a square. Beginning at the point of the pyramid is a street which goes round and round until it makes its way to the bottom. It is a long street! But alongside that street is a canal, an aqueduct that carries water from the throne of God which is at the apex of that pyramid. The water that proceeds "out of the throne of God" (22:1) flows along that street. When you have water, vegetation will grow. Along that watercourse grows a tree that bears fruit every month. Now what is the purpose of that tree? Fruit is for just one purpose, to be consumed. What was the first thing God gave Adam after He gave him Eve? He gave him fruit to eat. John adds that the leaves of the tree were for the healing of or for the sustaining of the nations. In the Garden of Eden man could eat, but they didn't have to eat in order to stay alive. Before Adam fell, there was no corruption or death in his body. God said Adam could partake of every fruit of the tree except one. This seems to have been for Adam's enjoyment—not to keep body and soul together, but to provide a basis of fellowship. After all, when you want to have fellowship with somebody, what do you do? You eat together. God will provide a basis for fellowship together.

This fruit does something else. In partaking of this fruit one memorializes that God is his constant source of provision. God provides the possibility of eating so that in that eating we will commemorate the fact that He is our manna, our living bread, and He sustains us throughout eternity. What John is emphasizing in his description of this city is that whereas cities began because men were in rebellion against God, now men are together in a city because they are subject to God. Men by nature are gregarious animals. There is a need in every individual for someone else. God recognized that in Adam. That's why He gave Eve to Adam. We need each other, and it is sin that has driven man from men. When we are at home with the Father, we will enjoy living as neighbors. We will be brought into the Father's presence. We will be at home with Him and in the company of all the redeemed of all the ages. We will behold God's glory and be protected and preserved by Him. The home will be a permanent home of indescribable beauty because it is filled with God's presence. It will be a place of safety and security, where we dwell without fear and where for the unending ages of eternity we will be sustained by God's provision. "Eye hath not seen, nor ear heard, neither have entered into the heart of man, the things which God hath prepared for them that love him" (1 Co 2:9).

We understand so little because we see now through a glass darkly, but then we shall see Him face to face, behold His glory, share His home, enjoy His bountiful provision forever.